More DOS Secrets

by Dan Gookin and Robert Mullen

Edited by Gretchen Lingham
Cover illustration by Lisa Mozzini
Art direction by Leah Steward-Shahan

Every effort has been made to supply the most current
information regarding the software publishers and products
discussed in this book. However, CPE assumes no
responsibility for any infringements of patents or other
rights of third parties which would result.

First Edition Copyright © 1992
Computer Publishing Enterprises
P.O. Box 23478
San Diego, CA 92193
Toll Free (800) 544-5541

Entire contents Copyright © 1992 by Computer Publishing Enterprises.
All rights reserved. No part of this publication may be reproduced
in any form or by any means, electronic or mechanical, including
photocopying, recording, or by any information storage or retrieval
system, without permission from the publisher.

Trademarked names appear throughout this text. Rather than provide a list of
trademark holders, or use trademark symbols to denote trademarked names,
the publisher and author acknowledge the trademarks and are using them for
editorial purposes only. No intention of trademark infringement is intended
upon any trademarked name appearing in this text.

0-945776-28-4
10 9 8 7 6 5 4 3 2 1

"The most unfortunate
thing that can happen to anyone is
that they limit themselves by becoming
afraid to try anything new."

One who tries to live by this

Acknowledgements

The authors would like to thank Gretchen Lingham and everyone at CPE for their hard work and patience while prying this book manuscript out of authors' hands. Thanks also go to Bill Neuenschwander at LaserMaster for graciously providing an outstanding WinPrinter 800 laser printer for evaluation purposes.

Table of Contents

Introduction	**xiii**

Chapter One: *Managing Memory on a '386, '486, '586* . . . **1**

    Being Conventional 1
    The Upper Crust 3
    Expanded Memory 5
    Extended Memory 5
    What Happens to Your Memory? 6
        Where It Goes, and Why 7
    The MEM Command 7
    TSRs and Device Drivers 10
    HIMEM.SYS 11
    What Is DOS=HIGH,UMB? 12
    LOADHIGH vs DEVICEHIGH 12
    Before You Invite It in, Ask It How Much It Eats . . 15
    The Best of EMM386.EXE 15
        Using UMA Without Creating
            Expanded Memory 16
        Using EMM386.EXE to Enable Your
            Weitek Coprocessor 16

Chapter Two: *Keyboard Enhancement*   **19**

    Using ANSI.SYS to Control Your Keyboard 19
        Interesting Key Reassignments 20
    The DOSKEY Command 23
        DOSKEY's Command Line History 24
            Reviewing Commands 25
            Editing Commands 26
        Multiple Commands With DOSKEY 26
        DOSKEY's Macros 27
        Useful DOSKEY Macros 28
            Quickly List the Contents of the
                Current Directory 28

```
                 Clear the Screen  . . . . . . . . . . . . . .  28
                 Format a Diskette That Doesn't Match
                    the Drive It's In . . . . . . . . . . . . .  28
                 Clear TEMP Files From Your
                    WINDOWS\TEMP Directory . . . . . . .  29
                 Macro Commands . . . . . . . . . . . . . . .  29
```

Chapter Three: *Disaster Recovery* 31

```
                 Things to Remember . . . . . . . . . . . . . .  31
                 Using the MIRROR Command . . . . . . . . . .  32
                    Undeleting Files With MIRROR  . . . . . . .  32
                 Undeleting a File  . . . . . . . . . . . . . . .  33
                 Unformatting a Disk . . . . . . . . . . . . . .  34
                 Disk Partitions  . . . . . . . . . . . . . . . .  35
                 Rebuilding the Partition Table . . . . . . . . .  36
```

Chapter Four: *Hiding and Securing Private Files* 39

```
                 Undercover File Activity  . . . . . . . . . . .  39
                    Using the ATTRIB Command . . . . . . . . .  40
                    Viewing Files and Their Attributes
                       Without ATTRIB . . . . . . . . . . . . .  43
                 That's All She Wrote (Microsoft, That Is) . . . . .  44
                 Securing Important Files  . . . . . . . . . . .  44
```

Chapter Five: *Setting Up a RAM Disk* 47

```
                 What's a RAM Disk All About? . . . . . . . . .  47
                 Installing a RAM Disk . . . . . . . . . . . . .  48
                 Making Your Programs Fly . . . . . . . . . . .  51
                 Self-Erasing Junk Files . . . . . . . . . . . .  51
```

Chapter Six: *Programming in DEBUG* 53

```
                 How to Program in DEBUG  . . . . . . . . . .  53
                 Creating a DEBUG Program Script . . . . . . .  54
                    Examining Your Work . . . . . . . . . . . .  55
                 Debugging the Program  . . . . . . . . . . . .  58
```

Contents

Chapter Seven: *Using PC Graphics* — 61

    PC Graphics Displays 61
    Using the MODE Command 63
    The Screen Dump 65
    Printing Graphics 66
    Printing Graphics and Text Using the
        Print Screen Key 67
    Printing Files With GRAPHICS.COM 67
    Graphics Files Translation Utilities 68
    Screen-Capture Utilities 70
    Some Parting Thoughts 71

Chapter Eight: *Computer Communications* — 73

    Connecting to a Modem 73
    Calling a BBS 75
    Using the CTTY Command 75
    Using CTTY for Security 77
    What's Out There 78

Chapter Nine: *Using Your Printer* — 81

    Printing From DOS 81
    DOS Printer Setup 82
    Printing With DOS 83
    Printer Control in the Editor 85

Chapter Ten: *Hard Drive Lessons* — 89

    Thought Processes 89
    Directory Ordering for Speed 91
    Easy Housekeeping 93
    Backing Up Your Files 94
    Taking It Seriously 99

Chapter Eleven: *Mondo Batch Files* — 101

    Formatting Disks 101
    Moving Files 102

Backup Checking	103
An AUTOEXEC.BAT Menu	105

Chapter Twelve: *HELP Yourself* — 109

Using DOS 5.0's HELP Facility	109
Using DOSSHELL's HELP	111

Chapter Thirteen: Windows *Secrets* — 115

Graphical Computing	115
Windows Modes of Operation	116
Real Mode	116
Standard Mode	116
'386 Enhanced Mode	117
Which Mode Is for Me?	117
Controlling the Windows	119
Selecting Wallpaper	119
Making Your Own Wallpaper	120
The Hard Way	120
Working With Windows	121
Opening Windows	122
Moving Windows Around	122
Recessing Your Windows	122
Scrolling Inside Windows	122
Maximizing Windows	123
Minimizing Document Windows	124
The Dialog Boxes	124
The Amazing Clipboard	125
Using the Clipboard's Contents	126
What the Clipboard Can Hold	126
Clipboard Files	127
Clearing the Clipboard	128
Looking Into It	128
Uses for the Clipboard	129
Working With DOS Programs	129
Using the DOS Prompt Icon	129

Contents

Not Enough Environment Space?	130
Changing Your DOS Prompt	130
Operating Modes and DOS Programs	131
Using Standard Mode	132
Using '386 Enhanced Mode	132
Some Pitfalls	132
DOS TSRs	133
Using Handy Utilities	134
Application Switching	135
Data Transfer and Non-*Windows* Programs	135
Copying Text and Pictures	135
Copying Pictures of the Screen	135
Some Insights Into Memory Usage	136
What Can Go Wrong	137
Good Thinking	137
Risky Business	138
Switching From Non-*Windows* Programs	138
Getting More on Your Screen	139
800-by-600 Mode	140
1024-by-768 or 8514/A Mode	143
Hardware Enhancements	144
Swapfile Virtues	145
How Much Is Enough?	147
Appendix: *All About ASCII Characters*	**151**
Control Characters	151
Standard Text Characters	151
Extended ASCII Characters	152
Control Character Names	153

Introduction

This book's parent work, *DOS Secrets*, packed a lot of information into a tiny, convenient space. The response was overwhelming; people loved reading "all the good stuff" without being bothered by meandering filler. With *More DOS Secrets*, we've tried to continue that effort, expanding on the information offered in *DOS Secrets* while still presenting it in the same tight, useful manner and without removing any of the insight or humor.

More DOS Secrets also contains vital information for PC users of the '90s. You'll find valuable material here on memory management, data recovery, system security, graphics, computer-to-computer communications, using your printer, improving system performance and dealing with Microsoft *Windows*. This is all in addition to the "cool stuff": information about using DOS's cryptic DEBUG program and plenty of helpful batch files. How could we pack so much information into one tiny book and at such a cheap price? *We must be crazy*!

What Level User?

Like its predecessor, *More DOS Secrets* is intended for experienced DOS users. If you're a beginner, we'd like to recommend the *Beginner's Guide to DOS*, also from CPE. That will get you up and running. Then you can turn to *DOS Secrets* and *More DOS Secrets*. Nothing here is too advanced. Don't be afraid to try something. But if the DOS prompt frightens you, *Beginner's Guide to DOS* is where you should really start.

Our Newest Author

This edition of *More DOS Secrets* welcomes a new co-author to the fold. Bob Mullen contributed heavily to this manuscript, coming up with all the ingenious hints and tips plus the special graphics and *Windows* information you'll find in the latter chapters. I thank Bob for his contributions, talent and wit—and I'm sure you will too as you sit up, power on your PC, open this book in your lap, and get ready to learn *More DOS Secrets*.

Dan Gookin
June, 1992

Chapter One
Managing Memory on a '386, '486, '586...

Memory management. Now there's a term you didn't see a few years back, especially with regard to DOS. But since DOS version 5.0 came out, memory management is an issue. We must deal with it. This chapter opens the closet door on memory management, introducing you to the subject if you're unfamiliar, and telling you how to deal with the memory management issues all PC users must face in the '90s.

In most of this chapter, everything we'll say about memory and memory management will be about the '386 and higher microprocessors. If you don't have one of the '386 "family" of computers, there really is no such thing as DOS memory management on your computer. Not being the cruel type, we've placed the discussion of memory management on older '286 (and primitive 8088/ 8086) computers at the end of this chapter.

Being Conventional

If there is any one subject that confuses people, it's memory. In truth, software manuals don't explain it, books don't delineate and the hardware vendors often don't know about it. To clarify memory in your mind so you can at least get the biggest and most profound differences, you have to break it down into very simple terms.

First of all, memory must be understood based on what you are talking about. At this highest level of understanding, there are two kinds of memory: hardware and software.

Hardware memory is a collection of little integrated circuits mounted either on your system board or an add-on memory board. This is something you can see and touch. When you hear people talking about RAM, SIMMs, SIPs, etc., in any size configuration and/or speed, you are hearing about hardware.

As far as memory goes, hardware memory is nothing more than a bunch of empty buckets designed to hold your data once the computer is turned on. Buy as much of this type of memory as you can afford and make that RAM as fast as your system can handle. That's the hardware side of memory.

What you do with hardware memory—all those empty buckets—is called memory management. This is the software side. Granted, this sounds a little nebulous, but it's really all about caring for your applications' needs. There are a lot of terms used when we talk about memory, but as far as your software (word processors, spreadsheets, etc.) is concerned, there is only one kind of memory . . . its own preference. Your software doesn't give a wit about all the differences in memory or even what the speed of the memory is. All it cares about is where it can find the memory it needs, and how much it has to work with.

You care for your application's memory needs with memory management software. Memory management systems or programs are software-based. As long as your computer hardware is compatible, you have options for memory management.

Hardware Compatibility

And what is hardware compatibility? It's actually known as the LIM standard. LIM stands for Lotus-Intel-Microsoft, the three big jujus of the computer industry (minus IBM). They developed a DOS memory standard called EMS, the Expanded Memory System. That's the key to unlocking memory management for all DOS computers, regardless of their microprocessor.

Keep that in your head, and you'll never be confused about memory management again.

How much memory is enough? Read the documentation for the software you intend to use most. Then buy as much memory as you can swing, and plug it into your computer. Your software will want to use either expanded or extended memory. If it doesn't specify which type of memory it wants, then it needs conventional memory. That's the basic memory available in all PCs.

Programs that will only use conventional memory (below the 640K mark) are becoming few and far between these days. Just as well: These are usually the programs that cause problems. Some of them actually insist on using specific ranges of memory below 640K. The nerve! But that was then and this is now. Most programs written in the '90s have adjusted to the modern concept of co-habitation, and are designed to run with other programs . . . without engaging in electronic fisticuffs over memory.

Being conventional means more than just being "mediocre." Conventional memory is the segment of system memory located below the 640K mark. Most of your DOS software wants to use conventional memory for its living and work space.

The Upper Crust

The area of memory located just above conventional memory is called the Upper Memory Area (UMA). The UMA is reserved by DOS for the computer's guts. That memory is taken up by ROM chips—not readable/writable RAM chips. For example, the system BIOS, your video memory, BASIC on IBM computers, the hard disk controller—all that complex stuff lives in the UMA.

Don't let the UMA confuse you (especially with Uma Thurman). The UMA was a secret with DOS. No one touched it and, therefore, most of it remained unused. All that memory space—some 384K—was marked "forbidden" by DOS. Yet free memory is good memory. When you learn that there is memory that DOS was keeping from you, don't you feel cheated? How can that unguarded memory go unused—especially if you need all the memory you can squeeze out of your '386, '486 or '586 system?

Before the advent of DOS 5.0, you had to buy a special software product in order to make use of the free, reserved memory in the UMA. These software products are called Program Loaders. One such program loader is Qualitas' *386MAX. 386MAX* not only finds free UMA space, it places your mouse drivers and other small programs (like TSRs), which would normally take up conventional space, in the UMA.

Program loaders as a whole reduce the waste of free UMA memory by analyzing free space and matching programs to the free segment of UMA that is closest in size to the program you want to put there. Remember how parking lots used to have spaces for small, mid-size and large cars to make best use of space?

If you upgrade to DOS 5.0, you don't have to buy a program loader, but DOS 5.0 doesn't minimize wasted space when it loads programs in the UMA. In order for EMM386.EXE to load programs into the UMA to save conventional memory space, you need to make sure that these statements appear in your CONFIG.SYS file before any other statements:

```
DEVICE=HIMEM.SYS
DEVICE=EMM386.EXE NOEMS
DOS=HIGH,UMB
```

The first line in the example loads the HIMEM.SYS device driver. This program controls all the extra memory in your '386 system. Installing HIMEM.SYS is the first step in DOS's memory management scheme. HIMEM.SYS creates a special "bank" of memory called the HMA or High Memory Area. That's an extra 64K of memory DOS can immediately put to good use.

(If you have extra memory [above one megabyte] in your '386, it's all extended memory. Yup, we did claim that expanded memory was what you really want. However, all '286 and later microprocessors with extra memory in them have extended memory. This may seem confusing, but bear with us for a second.)

The second line above tells DOS to load the EMM386.EXE memory manager. Here, EMM386.EXE is set up with the NOEMS switch. This directs the memory manager to use only the UMA, wresting control of that memory area from DOS's greedy "forbidden" arms.

The third line tells DOS to load itself into the HMA—that extra 64K of memory HIMEM.SYS creates. Instantly, this setup has saved you some 43K of memory; with DOS in the HMA you have more RAM to run your software. Additionally, the third line opens a link between the UMA and DOS's guts. Now, officially, the UMA is available for program storage.

Expanded Memory

When most DOS programs want extra memory, they need *expanded memory*. This is radically different from the *extended memory* native to all '386 family PCs. But there is a catch: Using DOS's EMM386.EXE device driver (or a similar third-party program) you can secretly convert some of your extended memory into the more useful expanded memory, which your programs probably want more than anything.

To make expanded memory available, you need to change one of the memory management commands in CONFIG.SYS. Specifically, you need to add the RAM option to EMM386.EXE, replacing the NOEMS option listed earlier in this chapter:

    DEVICE=EMM386.EXE RAM

The above command does everything it did before, but now 256K of expanded memory has been made available. In effect, 256K of extended memory has been converted into expanded memory. (This trick only works on '386 family computers; older systems are plum out of luck on this one.)

If you want more memory, follow the RAM option with a value in kilobytes. Specify as much memory as you like, but not more than you currently have. The rest of your memory will remain as extended memory, available for those programs that want it.

The sticking point here comes with *Windows*. *Windows* hates expanded memory with a passion. Instead, *Windows* wants extended memory—all of it. If you're running *Windows*, use the NOEMS option instead of RAM. Otherwise, *Windows* refuses to run in its ultra keen, '386 Enhanced mode. (More information on *Windows* is provided in Chapter Thirteen.)

Extended Memory

Well, here we are at the latest and greatest of the memory management systems for DOS: extended memory. Extended memory is the normal state of your computer's memory banks. XMS (eXtended Memory Specification) is the name of the standard document that proscribes the use of standard extended memory for the PC. A lot of people use the term XMS when they really mean "extended memory."

Extended memory is a lot simpler and runs a little faster than its confused-with companion, expanded memory. It's simpler because extended memory only deals with real addresses—not fictitious ones—and faster because it doesn't have to play charades with pages of memory and bank-switch them for segments of memory above 1024K.

Expanded memory is klutzy. It has to be, since it's the memory solution for all PCs and all DOS programs. To be compatible, it has to be simple. It's also extremely convoluted, accessing great quantities of memory in little bits and pieces—kind of like moving your house one box at a time. On the happy side, expanded memory is more useful under DOS. Keep that in mind when we rail against expanded memory in the future.

Extended memory is kind of like a large parking lot where all of the spaces are numbered. Each location in your memory chips has a finite address, much like a parking lot space does. Make no mistake, system memory over one megabyte is extended memory by default because it's an address-based system just like conventional memory. Extended memory needs a manager to access the addresses above 1024K, but otherwise you should think of extended memory as just so much more conventional memory. The addresses go on up to the limit of either your system's capabilities (a possible 4 gigabytes on any one system) or your wallet's, whichever comes first.

Extended memory is managed by an extended memory manager like the one included with DOS 5.0 and *Windows*, HIMEM.SYS. You can buy third-party products that do the same thing, but you may not get much better results than you would by just using HIMEN.SYS.

What Happens to Your Memory?

In the "old days," memory was not the bed of roses it is today. Programs used to step on each other's toes. TSRs and application programs used to duke it out for the same memory space all the time. When one of these cannibals lost, the system often crashed. Even today, in the *Windows* environment, the most common source of memory problems that can cause you serious grief is that dreaded denizen-of-the-deep, the General Protection Fault. You'd think these software vendors would have learned how to make their products dance together without injury by now.

Where It Goes, and Why

When a program is terminated (you decide to exit for one reason or another), the program is supposed to release the memory it has asked the memory managers for during the work session.

It is supposed to terminate itself and release the memory it occupies just to run, as well as the memory address it has requested from the memory managers for the temporary storage of its files. Many programs do this cleanly. Other greedy programs don't release all the memory they should, leaving you with wasted memory space.

There is an easy way to identify such programs by measuring your free memory capacity before and after you run the suspect program. You simply check on your available free memory space using DOS's MEM.EXE utility before and after you run the suspect program. By noting the difference in memory space used before and after the program is run, you'll quickly be able to pinpoint a poorly written program.

The MEM Command

If you're constantly running low on memory even when you shouldn't be, try using the MEM.EXE utility.

At the DOS prompt, type this:

MEM /C : MORE

You should see a list of the programs that have occupied your memory and where they are living. Below is a list of memory-resident programs (TSRs) for my computer when I ran the MEM command (your lists will most likely be a lot different):

8   Managing Memory On a '386, '486, '586 . . .

Conventional Memory :

Name	Size	in Decimal	Size in Hex
MSDOS	15952	(15.6K)	3E50
HIMEM	1072	(1.0K)	430
EMM386	3232	(3.2K)	CA0
SMARTDRV	2464	(2.4K)	9A0
COMMAND	2624	(2.6K)	A40
win386	3280	(3.2K)	CD0
CCBACK	5520	(5.4K)	1590
CCBACK2	82704	(80.8K)	14310
WIN	1600	(1.6K)	640
COMMAND	2832	(2.8K)	B10
FREE	533664	(521.2K)	824A0

Total FREE : 533664 (521.2K)

Upper Memory :

Name Size in Decimal Size in Hex

— More —

(This is when you press any key to display more information.)

Upper Memory :

Name	Size	in Decimal	Size in Hex
SYSTEM	167472	(163.5K)	28E30
win386	38464	(37.6K)	9640
MOUSE	17072	(16.7K)	42B0
STACKER	29776	(29.1K)	7450
CPCSCAN	9264	(9.0K)	2430

Total FREE : 0 (0.0K)

Total bytes available to programs
(Conventional+Upper) : 533664 (521.2K)
Largest executable program size : 533440 (520.9K)
Largest available upper memory block : 0 (0.0K)
7340032 bytes total contiguous extended memory
0 bytes available contiguous extended memory
1048576 bytes available XMS memory
DOS resident in High Memory Area

Managing Memory On a '386, '486, '586 . . .

Write down the Conventional Total Free amount and the Upper Total Free amount, as your before numbers. Run the suspect program, open and close a few bigger files and then terminate the application normally. Don't reboot the machine or use Ctrl-C or Ctrl-Break to terminate the program or batch file.

Now run the command:

MEM /C | MORE

one more time. Subtract the numbers you calculated after you ran the suspect application from the numbers you got before you terminated the offender. If you end up with a positive number, then the suspect application stands convicted of premeditated memory hogging. The convict is not releasing memory properly, and could cause you to run out of memory on occasion when you have no reason to run out at all.

Just think, this is only one of the programs that you run. Several could be messing up the same way. You won't know unless you check. Just in case you're curious, I'll explain what each segment of the command does.

The MEM part of the command invokes the DOS MEM.EXE utility program, which tells you what programs are loaded into memory and the amount of space they take up.

The /C (Classify) part of the command line tells MEM.EXE to break out conventional memory (below 640K) verses upper memory (from 640K and up).

The pipe symbol (SYMBOL 166 \f "Bembo" \s 12 \h) tells DOS to redirect or send the output of MEM /C to MORE (MORE.COM, which is probably in your DOS subdirectory) so that the information can be viewed one page at a time.

If you're the nutsy-boltsy type, you can substitute /P (Program) for the /C command-line switch to get even more detail about your system's memory. If you like to look at your nuts and bolts with a micron telescope, you may want to try substituting /D for the /C or /P command-line switch. The /D (Debug) command-line switch shows you just what your computer is thinking about in great detail. I should try this on my spouse.

TSRs and Device Drivers

The big benefit to TSRs is that you only load them once during each operating session. If you're going to invoke a program several times during a work session, it makes sense to make the program a TSR so you don't have to wait to load the program every time you need it. When you load a TSR, it allocates whatever memory it needs to occupy when it's resident.

A TSR, also called a memory-resident program, is a program that stays in memory after it's finished running, for example, the mouse driver, a time clock, or a pop-up utility like Borland's famous *SideKick*. TSR stands for the programmer's instruction that creates such applications. It means Terminate but Stay Resident. Why they use this instead of "memory-resident programs" baffles me.

Since a TSR is made in two parts (more later), when the second part (the actual program) terminates, it keeps the memory that it has been allocated so it has a place to live when you invoke the TSR again. If it didn't save memory in this way, you might load something else into the memory of your system that takes the space needed by the TSR when you want to run it.

Just about every program that you load into your CONFIG.SYS file will be a device driver of some sort. Most TSRs will be device drivers, too. Only the programs that are totally device-independent will be true stand-alone TSRs. TSR programs are intended to be loaded into system memory, and to stay there until you physically remove them or you reboot the machine.

Programs that operate hardware in the foreground or the background are becoming the dominant TSRs, because more of us are multitasking these days. We can run that fax, voice mail or network card in our systems with '386s or higher without maxing out our systems.

TSRs are made up of two essential elements. The first component is the part that loads the TSR, either from a batch file or from the DOS prompt itself. DOS allocates all available memory to most TSRs (if they want it) just like it does any other DOS program. The second part of the TSR is the part that actually executes or runs when you want it to do something for you.

For years, the big TSR on the popularity block was Borland's *SideKick*. *SideKick* provided several useful utilities that could be invoked or executed with keystroke combinations like Alt-F or some similar combination. Like all TSRs, *SideKick* was allocated memory when it was loaded. The thing to remember is that TSRs keep their allocated memory even when they are hidden, or don't seem to be there.

This means that it's important to terminate a TSR normally, or as the maker intended. If you don't do this, the TSR never sends DOS the instruction to release the memory it has occupied. TSRs do this by issuing a call to interrupt 20H or by issuing the DOS function call 4CH. The programs must be terminated "normally" (by the means provided by the original programmer) to make occupied memory available to other programs.

HIMEM.SYS

It's true: You might not have to buy an extended memory manager because one comes with DOS 5.0 and *Windows*. The name of Microsoft's extended memory manager is HIMEM.SYS. HIMEM.SYS is run from your CONFIG.SYS file as the very first line item in the file. It reads like this:

    DEVICE=HIMEM.SYS

That's all there is to it. Once installed, the extended memory manager functions much as a parking lot attendant. When a program asks for a parking space for a file, the lot attendant checks availability and doles out spaces as they're requested. The lot attendant tracks all of the parking spaces and retrieves the contents whenever a program requests it. It's really very simple.

Before the days of DOS 4.0, it was pretty much up to the software developer to worry about grabbing and holding memory for use by his or her applications. This means that some products used memory management techniques foreign to standardized software products today.

HIMEM.SYS has some obscure command-line options or parameters that you can use to control it. I have to confess, I never use these command-line options because they're designed to solve problems that can occur if you are running old DOS-based products. Some older programs actually compete with HIMEM.SYS to try to manage memory, as they would have back when HIMEM.SYS didn't exist. You'll be giving yourself a break if you choose not to run old programs.

Since the Microsoft memory managers and other utilities are released with every version of DOS and *Windows*, use the latest version from either software package. If in doubt, check the file creation date for each file on the diskettes that came with the original software. The later the date, the better. Don't forget to refer to the documentation that relates directly to the version you've opted to use!

What Is DOS=HIGH,UMB?

If you seem to be low on memory but you actually have gobs available (a gob is defined as four megabytes), you need to look at the way your system boots up.

The command-line statement

DOS=HIGH,UMB

causes DOS to load itself into the High Memory Area (HMA) each time you boot your machine. It appears in your CONFIG.SYS file if you've installed DOS 5.0. It should be the third line in your CONFIG.SYS file, the first being DEVICE=HIMEM.SYS, and the second being the DEVICE=EMM386.EXE statement.

To simplify this DOS=HIGH,UMB ditty, I'll break it down into segments. DOS=HIGH tells DOS to load itself into the HMA. The HMA is the first 64K above the 1024K mark. DOS does well there because this portion of your system's memory is little used, so there is no competition.

LOADHIGH vs DEVICEHIGH

Both of these commands are used to place programs and drivers into the UMA. By loading your programs and drivers high, you free up space in your conventional memory, or memory space located between 0 and 640K.

Even if you have 4 gigabytes of memory, you should still load all your drivers and some TSRs into your UMA, because some of your DOS-based programs will not be able to use expanded or extended memory. This leaves them only conventional memory to work with, so you want to give them as much space as you can to avoid those dreaded "Out of Memory" messages.

Both commands place programs into the UMA, but each of the commands must be used from different files. The DEVICEHIGH= command is used to load device drivers into the UMA from the CONFIG.SYS file. Here is a sample CONFIG.SYS file with the DEVICEHIGH= statement used to load drivers into the UMA:

```
DEVICE=HIMEM.SYS
DEVICE=EMM386.EXE NOEMS
DOS=HIGH,UMB
DEVICE=SMARTDRV.EXE /E:16 /B:2048 /S
DEVICEHIGH=MOUSE.SYS /Y
DEVICEHIGH=C:\STACKER\SSWAP.COM C:\STACVOL.DSK
DEVICEHIGH=C:\CC\CPCSCAN.SYS 3E0 3 1
FILES=40
BUFFERS=10
BREAK=ON
FCBS=5
STACKS=0,0
DEVICE=EPSN.SYS 2
```

Notice that some of the statements in the sample CONFIG.SYS file begin with DEVICE=, and others begin with the much-daunted DEVICEHIGH= syntax. The reason for using one or the other is determined by the type of device driver. Most device drivers do not access or manage memory.

Some common device drivers should never be loaded into the UMA because they can change size while doing their jobs. You can limit the amount of space they take, but drivers like SMARTDRV.-EXE need at least 512K to work, so there's no way they can be loaded high and still be expected to give you any performance.

If you try to load a driver with the DEVICEHIGH= command and it doesn't fit into one of the free spaces in your UMA, you'll need to remove another driver from the UMA, or settle for loading

14 Managing Memory On a '386, '486, '586 . . .

the larger driver into conventional memory with the DEVICE= command. If you try to load a biggy into the UMA and it won't fit, DOS will load it into the conventional memory area without any involvement from you.

The LOADHIGH= command is used to load programs and TSRs into the UMA from the AUTOEXEC.BAT file, only. If you want to load a background program, like a fax program file so your fax board can send or receive faxes, you can load the appropriate EXE or COM file into the UMA. This will free up some conventional space for use by other programs. Here is a sample AUTOEXEC.BAT file that will show you how I load some of my stuff into the UMA:

```
ECHO OFF
SET TEMP=C:\WINDOWS\TEMP
SET TMP=C:\WINDOWS\TEMP
PATH=D:\;C:\DOS;D:\STACKER;C:\WINDOWS;C:\CC;C:\CC;
PROMPT $P $G
LOADHIGH MODEST MONITOR
CCBACK/N
C:
CD\WINDOWS
```

Check out which of the loadable programs get stuffed into the UMA. The sixth line in the sample batch file says: loadhigh modest monitor. In this command line, I'm telling DOS to send the MODESET.EXE file into the UMA, and to run a command-line parameter called MONITOR. These two files tell DOS and the driver for the Weitek Power for *Windows*' accelerated video board to switch the monitor into 800 by 600 mode on system startup. Since these two files don't grow when executed, they're safe to load into the UMA.

The seventh line in the sample file says: ccback/N. This statement loads the background program that runs my Complete PC Communicator board. The board allows me to receive faxes, phone messages and modem input completely in the background. I can't load this program high because it calls and executes other programs that wouldn't be able to fit into the remaining UMA space after I've loaded all my drivers. Of course, I didn't learn this until I talked to an actual human being in Tech Support. Which brings me to my next piece of advice:

Before You Invite It in, Ask It How Much It Eats

Some programs shouldn't be loaded high because they open other program files during the normal course of their duties, or they expand in size once loaded. Some programs and TSRs cannot be loaded high because they load other programs or TSRs to perform special or secondary background operations (like automatically printing a fax in the background).

Since the available memory in your UMA is often made up of segments too small for some programs and TSRs, your secondary programs and TSRs may not load properly—or fail to load at all. Most programs cannot be loaded into non-contiguous (non-adjacent) segments of memory. This is especially true on DOS-based applications that don't recognize UMA at all, and expect to find as much contiguous conventional memory as they need.

It's always wise to ask software vendors how much overhead a program or hardware product needs before you buy it. Overhead is a common term for the amount of memory space (and/or system resources in the case of a *Windows* program) that is needed to run a program properly. At least read the package before you buy; most software vendors list the requirements (and overhead) for their software to run properly.

Load your programs into the UMA in the order of their size, from largest to smallest. This will assure the best fit. DOS will seek the first free UMA space for the largest program, leaving the smaller spaces for other smaller programs. You'll waste less space and get more programs into your conventional memory area using this method. As always, the goal is to free as much conventional space as you can.

The Best of EMM386.EXE

The EMM386.EXE utility included with *Windows* and DOS 5.0 is a real boon. If you have an 80386 or higher, you can use it. If not, you'll need to purchase a comparable program.

EMM386.EXE has an interesting feature that allows people who run only *Windows* programs to load stuff into the UMA—without costing them any extended memory space (the kind *Windows* wants). EMM386.EXE normally appears as the second statement in your CONFIG.SYS file. There are three popular ways to use EMM386.EXE:

Using UMA Without Creating Expanded Memory

One way is to ask EMM386.EXE to manage the UMA, but to refrain from creating and managing any expanded memory above 1024K. Using EMM386.EXE in this way minimizes overhead and maximizes your use of conventional and UMA memory space. At the same time, it leaves your memory resources above 1024K untouched by the expanded memory management facility that's the real lion's share of EMM386.EXE's capabilities.

The statement must be in the second line of your CONFIG.SYS file, and should read like this:

DEVICE=EMM386 NOEMS

The NOEMS command-line parameter tells EMM386.EXE that it can't play in your system memory's yard above the 1024K mark. You only lose 3.1K of overhead (the amount of space EMM386.EXE takes when it's running) to gain up to 180K of otherwise unavailable UMA space. Such a deal! The real benefit is that you can load DOS into the HMA, device drivers into the UMA, and you don't give up any additional space for unwanted expanded memory. *Windows* power users eat this up.

Using EMM386.EXE to Enable Your Weitek Coprocessor

A coprocessor is a stand-alone processor that is intended to take over part of the workload of the CPU. There are video coprocessors that make your screen faster, I/O coprocessors that make your files migrate more quickly, and of course there are coprocessors that do complicated math for your CPU.

If you are working with a CAD or technical drawing package, or if you have a piece of equipment that utilizes a math coprocessor, then you can probably gain from the use of the mother of all coprocessors made by Weitek Corporation. This famous little chip costs a small bundle, but it improves the performance of any piece of software (that can recognize and utilize it) to do processor-intensive floating-point calculations (classically CAD). The Weitek unit has become so commonplace that you will find a socket for it on most '386DX or higher personal computers. Microsoft has included a command-line switch to turn it on for you when you boot up your machine.

This one couldn't be simpler. Place this command line in your CONFIG.SYS file as the second statement:

DEVICE=EMM386.EXE W=ON

If your Weitek coprocessor is not installed via your system BIOS when you use this statement during system startup, you'll get this message:

Weitek Coprocessor not installed

You can turn off your Weitek coprocessor the same way, but with a different parameter that reads:

DEVICE=EMM386.EXE W=OFF

Pretty tricky, those Microsoft programmers! It's too bad the command-line switch doesn't work if you've loaded DOS=HIGH. I suppose this little barb is not all that much of a constraint to the people who can benefit from the Weitek coprocessor. All things considered, this statement is a very tidy way to enable and disable a popular device without adding any of that dreaded overhead.

You can expect to see peripheral manufacturers, like those who produce PostScript laser printers, accessing the Weitek coprocessor in the near future, since a few already utilize the coprocessor built into Intel's DX and DX2 line of processors.

Chapter Two
Keyboard Enhancement

If you like touching your PC (and anyone using a computer touches it a lot), then the thing you'll be touching most often is your keyboard. Keyboards can be springy and responsive or spongy and slug-like. Keyboards are a hardware issue, and replacing one is easy (just remember to turn off the computer before plugging or unplugging it). On the software side, there are things you can do to make a keyboard more responsive—without an expensive hardware upgrade.

This chapter is about using your keyboard more effectively. This can be done with the ANSI.SYS device driver that controls your console (and the keyboard is one half the console; the screen being the other half) as well as the handy new DOSKEY utility included with DOS 5.

Using ANSI.SYS to Control Your Keyboard

ANSI.SYS is really useful for controlling what your monitor and keyboard do. As far as your keyboard is concerned, you can change the assignment of a character to a given key, as well as display a statement when you press a key—all through ANSI.SYS.

First, you need to load ANSI.SYS into your computer by including the following statement in your CONFIG.SYS file:

DEVICEHIGH=ANSI.SYS

Make sure you place this command into your CONFIG.SYS file after the first three lines. (Refer to Chapter One for boning up on "the first three lines" of CONFIG.SYS, as well as UMA and DEVICEHIGH.) Since DOS 5.0 lets you load device drivers into the UMA (Upper Memory Area, or the space between 640K and 1024K), try to do so whenever appropriate. If you use the

DEVICEHIGH= command instead of the DEVICE= command, ANSI.SYS will use up space in your UMA, not in conventional memory space (the area below 640K). If ANSI.SYS doesn't fit into your UMA, DOS will stuff it into conventional memory space without notifying you. Either way, you need to get ANSI.SYS loaded into memory in order to use it.

Interesting Key Reassignments

If you've already loaded ANSI.SYS from your CONFIG.SYS file, you can reassign keys so that you get a character different from the one shown on the key you press. The first thing you need to do is create a file into which you can put your key reassignment commands—you may want to reuse the commands you create to manage ANSI.SYS over and over again. Creating a text file to contain the commands will let you avoid having to retype them every time you want ANSI.SYS to change the output of a key or keys. The file you create must be a simple ASCII or text file. Many of today's executive word processors, like *Word for Windows* and *Word for DOS* can create ASCII text files. *Windows NotePad* and DOS's Editor (EDIT.COM) will work as well, and you could even use good old Edlin to make the file you need.

Open the editor and file name of choice, enter the commands and save the file in ASCII text format. To create a file that can contain your commands, you must use a text editor that will make an escape character for you. If yours can't—or you don't know how—just use DOS's Editor or the EDLIN program that came with DOS 5.0.

To enter the escape character with DOS's Editor, press Ctrl-P then Esc. This inserts the escape character, which looks like a left-pointing arrow (←) into your text. With EDLIN, type Ctrl-V followed by [to create the escape character. This is because [is actually Ctrl-[, the escape character. Weird, yes, but it works (and with all versions of DOS).

In the following example, we will be telling ANSI.SYS to substitute the value of one key's character (the ~ key, or ASCII value 126) for the value of another character (the ¼ symbol, or ASCII value 172), separated by a semi-colon. Even though you

Keyboard Enhancement 21

can perform keystroke reassignments from the DOS prompt, we'll create a text file with DOS's Editor so we can reuse the command lines in the future. We'll open DOS's Editor and use an example text file named KEYCAP.TXT to make the tilde (~) key display the ¼ symbol:

First, run EDIT.COM and KEYCAP.TXT by using this command line:

EDIT KEYCAP.TXT

Press the Enter key now. DOS's Editor program will open and create an empty text file for you called KEYCAP.TXT.

Press Ctrl-P, then Esc to make the ESC (escape) character you need at the beginning of the command line. Next, enter the character (in its ASCII value) you wish to replace, followed by a semicolon and the ASCII value of the character you want to see in its place. The example in the next figure shows you the command line to use in order to replace the tilde sign (~) with the one-quarter fraction symbol (¼).

Now select "File Save" from Editor's main menu to save the file as KEYCAP.TXT. Select "File Exit" and Editor will close, placing you back at the DOS prompt.

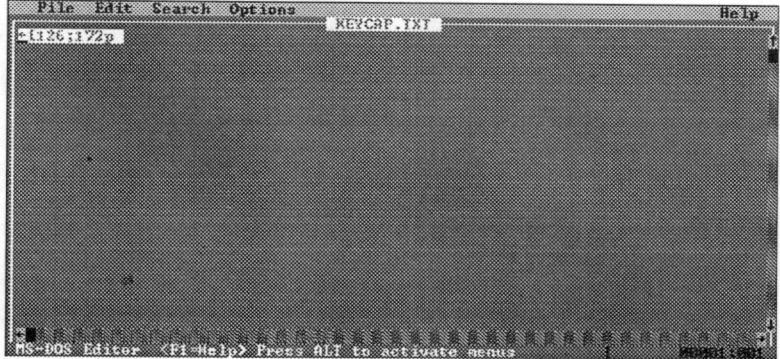

Figure 2.1: DOS's Editor and the contents of KEYCAP.TXT.

Congratulations! Now all you have to do is send the ANSI commands within KEYCAP.TXT to the ANSI.SYS driver to make it all happen!

Now type this syntax at the DOS prompt:

TYPE KEYCAP.TXT

That's about all there is to it. Every time you press the tilde (~) key, you'll now see the ¼ symbol instead. You can do a number of these key substitutions (if your text editor will accept the use of them) to create documents that include symbols like the ¼ symbol—which you might need for financial reporting, etc. Remember: You'll have to load ANSI.SYS and use the TYPE KEYCAP.TXT command every time you reboot, or you won't get the benefit of the keystroke reassignment the next time you start your computer.

You can substitute virtually any key for another key that has an ASCII value. Additionally, you can assign strings of text to certain keys. First, specify the ASCII value, then enter the string enclosed in double quotes like this:

←[0;59;"This is the F1 key"p

Above, this is what has been assigned to the F1 key, which is code 0;59. (The arrow is used to represent the escape character—however you enter it in your text editor.) Edit the KEYCAP.TXT file and add the above line, as well as the following:

[0;94;"dir";13p

Above, the DIR command is assigned Ctrl-F1. The extra ";13" tacks on an automatic press of the Enter key to the command. The following table lists the codes for the function keys F1 through F10:

Function Key Codes

Key	Unshifted	Ctrl	Alt
F1	0;59	0;94	0;104
F2	0;60	0;95	0;105
F3	0;61	0;96	0;106
F4	0;62	0;97	0;107

Keyboard Enhancement

Function Key Codes

Key	Unshifted	Ctrl	Alt
F5	0;63	0;98	0;108
F6	0;6	40;99	0;109
F7	0;65	0;101	0;110
F8	0;66	0;102	0;111
F9	0;67	0;103	0;112
F10	0;68	0;104	0;113

ANSI key reassignment is fun—and powerful. If you have a command you use often, consider assigning it to a function key or some useless key like ~. But there is a limit to this type of fun: Only DOS and a few programs will recognize the key reassignment. Most programs will ignore it. The reason is that programs extract keys from "deeper down" in the PC than DOS does. This skips over DOS and the ANSI.SYS driver.

The DOSKEY Command

DOSKEY is a TSR (memory-resident program) that enhances your DOS command line editing ability. DOSKEY comes with DOS 5.0, though you can get similar programs for older versions of DOS. Two popular ones are CED (Command EDitor) and DOSEDIT. Both are similar to DOSKEY, but are not covered here in any detail.

When loaded, DOSKEY itself occupies about 3K of memory space. It is a good candidate for loading into the UMA because of its smaller size. If you have the

    DOS=HIGH,UMB

command line in your AUTOEXEC.BAT file already, use the

    LOADHIGH=DOSKEY

command at the DOS prompt or in your AUTOEXEC.BAT file to load DOSKEY into the UMA. If there isn't enough room in the UMA, DOS will place it in conventional memory for you.

DOSKEY does a few different things for you: You can use it to execute a macro from the DOS prompt; you can use it to review commands after you've entered them; and you can also execute those commands as you review them.

DOSKEY creates a buffer that collects your command lines until the buffer fills. When you fill the buffer, DOSKEY pushes the oldest command out to make room for the newest command. You control the size of DOSKEY's buffer by telling DOS how much memory you want to dedicate to DOSKEY when you load it. DOSKEY.COM must be in the current directory, or else the name of the directory in which it resides must be in the path statement in your AUTOEXEC.BAT file so DOS can find and load it. The command to load DOSKEY should look like this:

DOSKEY

When you use the DOSKEY command without parameters, it is loaded with enough buffer space to hold about 512 bytes. If you don't have 512 bytes free, DOSKEY will set up a buffer size of 256 bytes, unless you specify otherwise. For DOSKEY's purposes, a byte is one character.

Most people don't feel the need to specify a smaller DOSKEY buffer, but you *can* specify how big you want the buffer to be. If you want to make the buffer very small because you're short on memory, but you still want to use DOSKEY, you can make the buffer half of the default size (for example) by using this statement:

DOSKEY /BUFSIZE=256

All you have to do is change the number following BUFSIZE= and the buffer will be created for the size you specify, assuming you have that much free memory available.

DOSKEY's Command Line History

DOSKEY will remember several commands for you, and allow you to review them by pressing the Up Arrow and Down Arrow keys. Let's try this one out. Go to the DOS prompt and load DOSKEY. You will see a message saying:

DOSKey Installed

Keyboard Enhancement

Type in this series of commands, just for fun:

cls
dir
command
exit
cls

Now press the Up and Down Arrow keys to see the commands you just entered in the order you entered them. If you work at the DOS prompt much, this can be a godsend—particularly for entering long strings of data that you would never remember otherwise.

The most common—and handy—use for DOSKEY is its command line history function. Press the Up Arrow and you can recall any of several previous DOS commands.

If you press F7, you'll see a list of recent commands, as many as will fit in DOSKEY's memory. F8 is a special "search" command. Type in the start of a command at the prompt, then press F8 and DOSKEY will match a previous command with what you've typed.

If you want to execute the commands again, just press the Enter key when the command you would like to execute becomes visible during the review process. Here's a more complete table of commands you can use to work with the DOS commands that DOSKEY has added to its "history" list:

Reviewing Commands

Keystroke:	What it Does:
F7	Displays the entire command history list.
Up Arrow	Displays previous command.
Down Arrow	Displays next command.
Pg Up	Displays oldest command.
Pg Dn	Displays newest command.
F8	Searches for command text typed in just before striking the F8 key. Displays that text if found.
F9	Displays command line from history list by history list line-item number.

Esc	Erases the displayed command.
Alt-F7	Deletes the history list.

You can also edit commands as you review them. The ability to edit commands kept on DOSKEY's history list can be invaluable if you need to change, say, one character in a long command that contains lots of command-line switches. You can edit the contents of a command line (like those command-line switches) by using one of the keystrokes from this next table:

Editing Commands

Keystroke	What it Does
Home	Moves cursor to beginning of command line.
Ctrl-Home	Deletes all characters left of cursor.
End	Moves cursor to end of command line.
Ctrl-End	Deletes all characters right of cursor.
Left Arrow	Moves cursor left one character.
Ctrl-Left Arrow	Moves cursor to beginning of current word.
Right Arrow	Moves cursor right one character.
Ctrl-Right Arrow	Moves cursor to beginning of next word.
Backspace	Moves cursor left one character. If cursor is at end of line, Backspace deletes one character to left of cursor.
Del	Deletes character at cursor.
Ins	Toggles Insert and Overstrike modes. Overstrike mode is the default.

Multiple Commands With DOSKEY

You can enter several commands on one command line if you've loaded DOSKEY first. You have 128 characters to work with on each line. By the way, one space also takes up one of your 128 characters, so judge accordingly.

To slap down more than one command at the DOS prompt, press Ctrl-T between them. For example, below are two DIR commands to list program files in the current directory:

Keyboard Enhancement

```
DIR *.COM /W ¶ DIR *.EXE /W
```

When you press Ctrl-T, you'll see a paragraph symbol (¶) on your screen, as shown above. That's what separates the two DOS commands. First DIR *.COM /W is executed, then DIR *.EXE /W follows. This is the same as typing the two commands at two separate DOS prompts—the Ctrl-T almost acts like an inserted Enter character.

The main drawback to this trick is that it only works at the DOS prompt. You cannot use Ctrl-T in your batch files. Also, you have to press Ctrl-C to cancel each command you've entered; above that's two Ctrl-Cs to cancel the two commands. Weird, but it's nice when you want to type several commands at once.

DOSKEY's Macros

If you want to run a particular series of commands more than once, you may want to create a DOSKEY macro. DOSKEY loads a sequence of commands (macro) into system memory, and runs them when you ask for them. DOSKEY macros are small files that can be stored in memory but not on disk. They are created by DOSKEY so you can reuse lengthy commands or complex multiple commands. A DOSKEY macro is limited to 127 characters in length. You simply need to create and store the macro.

The syntax for creating a DOSKEY macro is:

```
DOSKEY MACRONAME=COMMANDS
```

MACRONAME is, obviously, the macro name, and it can be anything—even a legitimate DOS command. The COMMANDS are things you'd type on the command line. If these include optional parameters, they're specified using the dollar sign: $1 is the first item, $2 the second, on up through $9. To specify all the options, use $*.

After you create the macro, you simply type the macro name in lieu of the command line sequence you want. It's a lot simpler and quicker. To illustrate the concept, here are some examples of useful DOSKEY macros.

Useful DOSKEY Macros

Here's a few DOSKEY macros that you may find useful. Let's start with some pretty simple macros and then continue into some fairly complex ones.

Quickly List the Contents of the Current Directory

To create a macro that lists the contents of the current directory, use the following syntax and then press the Enter key in order for DOSKEY to remember the macro in the future:

DOSKEY D=DIR

In this case, D is the MACRONAME you decided to give the macro, and DIR is the DOS COMMAND you want to use. After you type this syntax and press the Enter key, your computer will present you with a listing of the files in the current directory when you simply type the letter D.

Clear the Screen

One of the most popular commands used at the DOS prompt is the CLS or "clear screen" command. CLS wipes out anything on the screen and then places the DOS prompt at the top-left of the screen. Here's a simple macro that will do this for you:

DOSKEY C=CLS

This example is about as simple as DOSKEY macros get, but think about the possibility of formatting a whole box of 720K diskettes on a 1.44M drive—it would be a lot less tedious if you didn't have to remember and retype the syntax over and over again. With the next DOSKEY macro, you don't have to!

Format a Diskette That Doesn't Match the Drive It's In

Here we're going to create a macro that formats a 720K diskette in a 1.44 MB drive. This command will load DOSKEY and tell DOSKEY that the expression "FB" is equal to the expression "FORMAT B: /F:720". Drive B was used as the drive in this example, but you can substitute your drive designation if different:

DOSKEY FB=FORMAT B: /F:720

Keyboard Enhancement

You will only need to use this syntax to execute the previous, complex command line:

    FB

Clear TEMP Files From Your WINDOWS\TEMP Directory

If you're tired of having to clean up those unsightly "temp" files created by both DOS and *Windows* applications, use DOSKEY to run a quick ditty that shows you your *Windows* junk files, clears them out and then verifies that the junk is gone. The command won't erase any other valuable files that you might also keep in the TEMP subdirectory. (This might also be a good example of multiple commands on one line):

    CD\WINDOWS\TEMP ¶ DIR/P ¶ DEL ~*.* ¶ DIR/P

This is a command line-only special thing for DOSKEY alone. Here is a table of more commands used to create macros:

Macro Commands

Keystroke	What It Does
$G or $g	Redirects output to file or device, not display.
GG or gg	Adds output to the end of a file.
$L or $l	Redirects input from device or file, not keyboard.
$B or $b	Directs macro output to another command.
$T or $t	Separates commands on a command line.
$$	Designates the dollar sign character ($).
$1 though $9	Substitutes for parameters or switches.
$*	Indicates that new parameters or switches will be used instead of parameters or switches included in the macro.

Chapter Three
Disaster Recovery

Sooner or later, for some reason or another, we all find that the data on our hard drives is lost. Or at least it *seems* to be lost. If you rely on your computer for anything else besides game-playing, you really should provide yourself with some form of recourse should a serious problem arise.

This chapter discusses various ways to prevent and recover from common PC disasters. Of course, being careful is always the first and best rule of thumb. But when disaster strikes, you do have some tools at your disposal.

This chapter covers the popular DOS tools for breathing new life into a damaged—or simply deranged—PC.

Things to Remember

Without the aid of a file or disk management utility like *The Norton Utilities* or *PC Tools Deluxe*, using DOS 5.0's MIRROR is perhaps the easiest way to ensure that you'll be able to quickly recover data lost through accidental format or erasure. MIRROR creates an image of your hard drive's partition, boot information and file allocation table in your root directory. If you install it correctly, it will update this stored image with your hard drive's critical data every time you start up your computer.

Those *other* utilities mentioned above do the same thing in a similar manner. The basic fact of life in data recovery is that you must have a second set of critical system details stored on your hard drive if you want to get yourself out of hot water *quickly* at a future date.

You don't really need MIRROR to recover data files—depending on the circumstances. In fact, DOS 5.0 can recover most *individual* files as long as the subdirectory that once held the lost data still exists, and you haven't performed any file-saving since the lost file was deleted. On the whole, DOS 5.0's MIRROR and other disk management utilities allow you to take care of yourself much better than any previous versions of DOS.

Disk utilities included with DOS 5.0 offer ways to:

- Save the data on a disk or diskette that has been accidentally formatted.
- Save the data on a disk that has been mistakenly deleted.
- Retrieve lost data from a subdirectory that has been deleted.
- Rebuild a damaged partition table.
- Save all data in a directory or subdirectory that is no longer readable by DOS.

Using the MIRROR Command

You can save your butt someday if you just follow some simple steps to keep a *mirror image* of your vital system areas on your hard drive. To do this, you use a utility that comes with DOS 5.0 called MIRROR.COM. The MIRROR utility helps fight three types of disaster: general hard disk explosions and virus-inflicted damage to the hard disk boot sector; accidental formatting of vital disks; and the accidental deletion of files. Note that the emphasis here is on *accidental*; the MIRROR command doesn't help you much if you're careless.

Undeleting Files With MIRROR

While MIRROR doesn't undelete files, it helps you to do so in a painless manner. But remember: MIRROR can only recover what *can* be recovered. This means you must stop saving other files so that they are not saved (or copied) *over* the deleted file you want to recapture. If you do save another file over the deleted file you want to recapture, there's no utility in the world that can make your deleted file complete again.

To activate MIRROR's special undelete feature, use this syntax in your AUTOEXEC.BAT file:

Disaster Recovery

MIRROR /TC

This statement tells MIRROR to track files that you delete from drive C. If you want MIRROR to track another drive, like drive D as well as drive C, you would use this statement:

MIRROR /TC /TD

This syntax activates MIRROR's deletion-tracking facility for drive C with /TC and for drive D with /TD. This aids in file recovery on those two drives. If you want to use MIRROR on additional drives, stick their letters at the end of the line prefixed by a /T.

The file tracking ability of MIRROR is valuable because not only does it make a backup copy of your hard drive's critical data, but it also keeps track of files that have been deleted recently. This assures you of being able to save data lost by almost any honest mistake. Remember, MIRROR doesn't recover deleted files by itself, nor does MIRROR prevent files from being deleted. For that, you need other DOS utilities.

Undeleting a File

To undelete a file, you need to run DOS's UNDELETE.EXE program. MIRROR saves a record of your file-deletion activity; UNDELETE does the work of making a file useful again.

Most people don't realize this: When you delete a file, *the file does not go away!* DOS simply renames the file in a fashion that does not allow you to see it when you list your files using DOS. The file is still there, intact—with 91 percent of the file name still intact. You just can't see it under normal circumstances.

UNDELETE saves all of the deleted files for the current directory that both DOS and MIRROR know about. To restore deleted files whose information has been recorded by MIRROR, use this syntax:

UNDELETE

To see a list of all of the deleted files that could be recovered with UNDELETE, use this statement:

```
UNDELETE /LIST
```

If you want to undelete all files in a given directory, but let UNDELETE complete the file-naming process automatically, it will create new file names if there are any duplicates after undeleting. To do this, use this syntax:

```
UNDELETE /ALL
```

To tell UNDELETE to save *all* deleted files that have been tracked by MIRROR, use this syntax:

```
UNDELETE /DT
```

Most often, you'll use UNDELETE with the name of the file (or wildcard) you've just used with the DEL command. Imagine you just deleted COMMAND.COM by mistake. Yank it back to life with this command:

```
UNDELETE COMMAND.COM
```

If you just follow the instructions on the screen, soon your COMMAND.COM—or whichever file you've named, will be back from the dead. This command even works with wildcards:

```
UNDELETE *.BAK
```

Above, UNDELETE yanks back all your *.BAK files.

If any files cannot be recovered, the UNDELETE command will let you know. This is a dreadful situation, but it happens. Just be more careful next time, and be thankful that after five versions, DOS finally has its own UNDELETE command.

Unformatting a Disk

DOS 5.0 doesn't really destroy data when you format a disk unless you specifically tell it to do so. This concept is called "Safe Formatting." It's really a neat improvement for us no-brainers who are thinking about something else when we should thinking about the disk we're formatting.

You can unformat a disk that has been mistakenly formatted by using DOS 5.0's UNFORMAT.COM utility. You can't use it on network drives, but otherwise it's a great little utility for those of us who've accidentally formatted our backup diskette. When that happens, and assuming the disk is in drive A, type the following immediately after reformatting:

UNFORMAT A:/J

This also works if you—gulp!—accidentally reformat your hard drive. There are a billion warning messages to prevent you from doing that, but if you're really lazy, it's possible. You can recover your information with the UNFORMAT command:

UNFORMAT C:

Follow the directions on the screen and you'll soon have your disk back. It will take some time, and everything may not be normal. But it's better than starting all over. If you didn't use the MIRROR command, specify UNFORMAT's /U switch:

UNFORMAT C:/U

Disk Partitions

There's little mystery surrounding the dreaded Partition Table, and it's less interesting these days. Under early DOS versions, you could only partition a drive at 32 MB. This meant that those of us who were blessed with drives larger than that had to partition the drive to be multiple drives. You fooled DOS into believing everything was kosher by partitioning a 70 megabyte drive into three "logical drives" of 32 megabytes or less. Amazing how effective fooling DOS can be. What else is new?

There are other reasons for creating multiple partitions. If you're running OS/2 and DOS on the same computer, for example, you need to create a partitioned area for each because DOS and OS/2 have different ways of storing files on disk.

DOS's FDISK.COM groups contiguous (immediately adjacent) cylinders on a hard drive into a partitioned area or logical drive. These days, for system security reasons, network administrators seem to be the most likely candidates to opt for multiple partitions. In fact, it used to be popular to create multiple partitions and call each partitioned area a drive in itself so that you or others could not kill quite as much data if something went wrong. With the advent of DOS 5.0 and MIRROR.COM it's not quite so critical. You can usually save most of your valuable data if you take a few simple precautions.

Unless you run FDISK.COM and actually choose to delete or recreate a partition on your drive, odds are you'll never have to run FDISK.COM except when you install a new drive.

There are some viruses out there that specialize in garbling hard disk partition information, but occasionally your hard disk partition table may become corrupted. That's where UNFORMAT.COM comes in.

Rebuilding the Partition Table

Ever get this DOS message when you try to access a disk or hard drive?:

Invalid drive specification

Argh! It's time to run UNFORMAT.COM. UNFORMAT will restore drive partition information so that DOS can read your drive once more. The catch is that you must have run MIRROR.COM in order to have a backup record of your critical hard drive information on file to begin with.

Of course, you need to keep it on a floppy diskette in order to access the saved information once your partition has failed, since you won't be able to read the dead drive. When saving a copy of the partition table, MIRROR will ask you which floppy drive contains the diskette to receive the backup info file.

To save a copy of your partition table "just in case," add this line to your AUTOEXEC.BAT file:

MIRROR C:/PARTN

Now here is the statement to run when you need to restore that damaged partition info on your hard drive (in this case, drive C:) with UNFORMAT:

UNFORMAT C:/PARTN

Disaster Recovery

Like MIRROR, UNFORMAT asks you to insert the floppy diskette with the backup file so you can restore the old critical data on your hard drive. That should do it. If you save a copy of your partition table, root directory, boot sector and file allocation table using MIRROR.COM, you can save the day at that fateful hour when your computer seems to *lose* its hard drive on you. Not to mention those missing files that also seem to lose themselves!

Yikes! Hard drive messages are the worst. If you ever get a "Drive C? Drive C? We ain't got no stinkin' drive C!" type of error message, try these things:

1. Reset the computer. This may revive the hard drive in some cases.

2. Check your PC's SETUP program. Your hard drive "type" may be wrong or missing. (Refer to your dealer for the correct type, or call the manufacturer —a hassle, but it works.)

3. Run FDISK to confirm that a hard drive is really there. If FDISK can't find the hard drive, then you may have a mechanical problem. If FDISK identifies the drive as "unformatted" or "non-DOS," then run the UNFORMAT program as described above. Keep in mind this only works when you've first used MIRROR /PARTN.

Chapter Four
Hiding and Securing Private Files

You can keep files on your hard drive and arrange it so that others can't see them. This can be pretty handy on machines that are shared by many at the office. Who knows—maybe you can keep your updated resume on your boss's machine without your boss knowing it's there! Just kidding; don't try this at work.

This chapter is about DOS security. Up front, we're happy to tell you that DOS has little if no security. Hiding and securing files is possible to a limited extent. But keep in mind that anyone with the same knowledge can easily get at those files.

Undercover File Activity

Want to see whose resume is on *your* system? You can ask DOS to give you a directory of hidden files by craftily using this syntax:

    DIR /AH

This is what *you* may find when you use the above statement:

```
Volume in drive D has no label
Volume serial Number is 187A-6E6F

Directory of D:\
IO          SYS         33430 04-09-91
MSDOS       SYS         37394 04-09-91
FIREBOB     DOC          4044 06-02-92

3 files          74868 bytes
89,889,729 bytes free
D:\
```

Hoo boy! Better see just who's named in that "hidden" file. Somebody, and we're not saying *who*, decided to hide a file by changing the file attribute to *hidden*. And on your system, too! The nerve. So sorry, Bob.

Maybe this is the only copy of the memo; let's dump it. Let's delete the file with this statement at the DOS prompt:

DELETE FIREBOB.DOC

But DOS is too slick for you. This is what you get:

D:\ DEL FIREBOB.DOC
Bad command or file name

D:\

Hmmm! What's the buzz? That didn't work. I'll try this!

D:\ ERASE FIREBOB.DOC
File not found

D:\

Because you're working with a hidden file, you must change the *attribute* from "system" to archive; then you can delete the file using your favorite method. The way to do this is to use the ATTRIB command.

Using the ATTRIB Command

You hide files by changing their *attribute* to that of a *hidden* file. You already have hidden files on your computer. Critical files often have the hidden attribute set so you don't mistakenly move or delete them.

A good example of hidden files now located on your computer would be DOS's IO.SYS and MSDOS.SYS files.

If these files are moved or deleted, your system will not boot from that drive unless you replace them in exactly the same place with the same version of DOS. But enough of that.

To make a system/hidden file visible *and* erasable (as well as setting the archive attribute), use this next statement:

ATTRIB RESUME.DOC -H -S +A

Now you can erase that unwanted file.

Here's the syntax you should use to hide a file:

ATTRIB RESUME.DOC +H

Hiding and Securing Private Files

You can place the attribute designation after "ATTRIB" in the statement you use, or you can place it after the file name or wild card (*.*) statement. ATTRIB.EXE will work either way.

Remember to include the directory name where ATTRIB.EXE lives in your PATH statement, or DOS may not be able to find it when you try any of these command line statements!

You can hide all of the files in any directory by using this statement:

ATTRIB *.* +H

To make all hidden files in a directory appear as if by magic, use this syntax:

ATTRIB *.* -H

Don't forget to use the ATTRIB *.* +H statement to hide these files again or the cat will be out of the bag. Never let your boss know that there is a DOS guru in the house!

You can even redirect ATTRIB's output to other DOS commands. For example, you can use MORE.COM to display ATTRIB's output one page at a time, requiring you to strike any key in order to display the next page of information. Here's an example of how to display the attributes of a long list of files so you get to *read* the list! This is really useful on a '486 or higher, because these machines scroll so fast you haven't a prayer of reading a lengthy file listing without the help of MORE:

```
C:\DOS ATTRIB *.* | MORE
A  C:\DOS\APPEND.EXE
A  C:\DOS\ASSIGN.COM
A  C:\DOS\ATTRIB.EXE
A  C:\DOS\CHKDSK.EXE
A  C:\DOS\COMMAND.COM
A  C:\DOS\COMP.EXE

A  C:\DOS\DEBUG.EXE
A  C:\DOS\DISKCOMP.COM
A  C:\DOS\DISKCOPY.COM
A  C:\DOS\DOSHELP.HLP
 — More —
```

(This is when you press any key to continue.)

A C:\DOS\DOSKEY.COM
A C:\DOS\DOSSWAP.EXE
A C:\DOS\DRWATSON.EXE
A C:\DOS\DRWATSON.LOG
A C:\DOS\EDIT.COM
A C:\DOS\EDIT.HLP
A C:\DOS\EDLIN.EXE
A C:\DOS\EMM386.EXE
A C:\DOS\EQUIP.EXE
A C:\DOS\EXPAND.EXE
A C:\DOS\FASTOPEN.EXE

This statement lists all the file attributes and filenames in the current subdirectory, one screen's worth at a time. See how this works? You can send the output to another DOS command and process information further before it's displayed.

Try the following command to selectively list all attributes and filenames in, for example, the DOS directory *and every subdirectory under it!* We'll also ask ATTRIB to show the attributes of the files on the list, and FIND.EXE to sort out all but the file names that have the letters "EXE" in the file-name extensions. If you want ATTRIB to look at files in the current subdirectory *and every subdirectory below the current directory*, insert the /S switch into the statement after the file name or wildcard statement. The next example shows how you would use the /S switch:

ATTRIB *.* /S | FIND ".EXE"

Now this is what I get when I run this command; what *you* get for a file listing on your system will most likely be different, but the concept is the same:

A D:\STACKER\DRVTYPE.EXE
A D:\STACKER\INSTALL2.EXE
A D:\STACKER\SCHECK.EXE
A D:\STACKER\SCREXEC.EXE
A D:\STACKER\SCREXEC2.EXE
A D:\STACKER\SDEFRAG.EXE
A D:\STACKER\SDIAG_AT.EXE

Hiding and Securing Private Files 43

```
A D:\STACKER\SDIR.EXE
A D:\STACKER\SEDIT.EXE
A D:\STACKER\SREMOVE.EXE
A D:\STACKER\VIDTYPE.EXE
A D:\EMM386.EXE
A D:\SMARTDRV.EXE
```

Check out the last two file names on the list. Did you notice they're from other subdirectories? They're from the root directory in drive D:, which is where I was when I ran the command!

Viewing Files and Their Attributes Without ATTRIB

You can also view all files of a particular attribute using the DIR command. With DIR, you can screen files for viewing purposes, but you can't change the attributes. It's a pretty straightforward method, and easy to recall. Be sure you don't use a space between the switch (/A) and the attribute (R, A, S or H).

This is the syntax I used to see just the files with the attribute of hidden (/AH) in my root directory:

DIR /AH

This is what I got ...

Volume in drive D has no label
Volume Serial Number is 187A-6E6F
Directory of D:\

IO SYS 33430 04-09-91 5:00a
MSDOS SYS 37394 04-09-91 5:00a
386SPART PAR 10237952 04-26-92 12:11p
STACVOL DSK 108406784 02-23-92 7:41p
4 file(s) 118715560 bytes
4792320 bytes free

You can use any of these attributes from the next table *after* the **/A command line switch:

Attribute	What DIR Displays
H	Hidden Files.
-H	Files not Hidden.

S	System Files.
-S	Files other than System files.
D	Directories.
-D	Files, but not Directories.
A	Archive Files.
-A	Files ready for Archiving.
R	Read-Only Files.
-R	Files that aren't Read-Only.

That's All She Wrote (Microsoft, That Is)

DOS is not world-renowned for its system security. In fact, the contents of this chapter represent most of what can be done to secure files under DOS 5.0. Of course, the stalwart of you will come up with some pretty creative solutions. By redirecting output using the pipe symbol and other DOS commands on the same command line, you can get pretty cagey.

All in all, the management of file attributes is the meat (not the motion) of file security as far as DOS is concerned. Word is being strewn about that Microsoft will include some sort of security utilities in the next major upgrade to DOS. I for one am *not* holding my breath! Plan on using the tools called ATTRIB and DIR for some time to come.

Securing Important Files

Hiding files is cute, but ineffective. Anyone who knows DOS, the ATTRIB command, or DIR's /O switch can find them. Big deal. What's more important is protecting files. A great example took place while working on this book.

As Bob and Dan were swapping files, taking turns working on them, they'd exchange a disk with every file on it. But suppose we didn't want one file changed. To prevent it from being overwritten by an older version, we'd slap on read-only protection using the ATTRIB command. For example:

ATTRIB +R CHAP06.DOC

Hiding and Securing Private Files

Above, Chapter Six was protected with read-only access. That meant no other file named CHAP06.DOC could overwrite it—important when you're doing COPY *.DOC operations that can wipe out a whole gang of related files. Also, CHAP06.DOC couldn't be modified. While it could be loaded into the word processor and read, no changes could be written back to disk because the original file was protected.

To make the file available once again, read-only access was removed:

    ATTRIB -R CHAP06.DOC

Turning read-only access on for important files is a must, especially on busy systems used by two or more people, or when several files are being worked on at once.

Chapter Five
Setting Up a RAM Disk

A RAM Disk is a portion of your system's memory that has been allocated to the task of appearing to be another disk drive. Also called a *virtual* drive, a RAM disk looks like a very fast drive to your system because it's electronic in nature, not mechanical like most of the drives you and I use. There's no waiting for access times, caches, or read/write delays. A RAM drive or RAM disk operates at the speed of the system RAM where it lives. This means that the drive's access speed could be as fast as 50 or 60 nanoseconds, rather than the more prevalent 15 or 28 milliseconds on which mechanical drives operate.

This chapter is about using a RAM disk. RAM disks used to be playthings only the memory-rich could afford. The secret is that using a RAM disk can be a real speed booster. This chapter shows you how.

What's a RAM Disk All About?

Increasing speed is a great idea! But what does a RAM disk *do*? A RAM disk is an incredibly fast disk from where you can run your applications, if you have the space. It's also a great place to send your DOS and *Windows* TEMP files. You can also set up a disk cache on a RAM disk to improve the performance of your hard drives.

Your system will run a lot faster because it doesn't have to wait for a klunky hard drive to get off its hub and get to work—a RAM disk seems to be instantaneous. In a world where instant gratification is the prime mover, you don't know what you're missing if you haven't run a normally slow application from a RAM disk.

RAM disks can be a real boon by increasing your computer's apparent operating speed as well as serving other functions. The concept of a RAM disk is just this: You create a virtual (pretend) disk that resides in your computer's memory. You need *gobs* of memory to do this (here, "gobs" mean about two megabytes or more). You are, of course, limited by the amount of memory that you can dedicate to a RAM disk. That's the biggest *rub*, as they say. Fear not! Memory is getting cheaper these days. More and more people who make their living with computers justify the expense of the additional memory in the name of productivity.

There are a few shortcomings. The greatest drawback is that a RAM disk is volatile. It only remains in existence as long as your system is powered up or is not rebooted. If either of these events occur (accidentally or otherwise) you will lose the contents of a RAM disk.

Needless to say, with many *Windows* programs, initialization files need to be updated during many applications' installations. Several of the more advanced applications tell you to reboot or restart *Windows* in order to make the newly installed application fully operational. If you press the button to cause a reboot when you are prompted to do so, you may inadvertently erase the contents of your RAM disk. *This is the biggest single reason to keep data files on floppies or a hard drive while using a RAM disk.*

Installing a RAM Disk

To increase the speed of a program or programs, you can create a disk in memory that will hold your slower applications. With your programs on the slippery fast RAM drive, the computer will no longer have to wait for a mechanical hard drive to play catch up. DOS's RAM disk utility makes a logical, rather than a physical, drive in memory for you using the next available drive letter designation. In other words, if your highest drive letter designation is C:, your RAM disk will be created using D: as the RAM disk's letter name.

To illustrate how this is done, I'll show you how to install RAMDRIVE, convert some of your memory to a RAM disk, copy a desired program to the RAM drive, and then run the program from it. Before we do this, however, there are a few considerations we must make before actually creating a RAM disk.

Setting Up a RAM Disk

The first consideration is the size of the RAM disk. Make sure you *really do* have enough free RAM to spare for your RAM disk. If you're planning to copy a slow or disk-intensive program to the RAM drive, while still keeping your document or work files on a permanent media like your hard drive (recommended), you need to know if the application expands in size while being run. *Don't cut it close.* Give yourself five to 10 percent more space than you expect to use. If you run out of RAM drive space, your program may slow down again because it's saving periodically to the root directory of your boot drive when it runs out of RAM disk space.

Also, remember that if you're multitasking several programs at once, memory can get pretty scarce out there (especially for graphics file jockeys), and if you've allocated a big chunk to a RAM disk for one of your applications, the rest may starve for memory and start swapping to disk. These other hungry programs may slow your system down enough to offset the gain you made by running any application from a RAM disk. By the way, the DOS documentation tells us that 4 megabytes is the largest RAM disk size we can use. I've made RAM disks of 5 megs, so don't be put off. I haven't explored the ceiling in size, but it's greater than 4 megabytes. A little experimentation might be due here.

You can place a RAM disk in conventional, expanded or extended memory. A RAM disk in conventional memory means the size of the disk can't exceed 640K—minus what your system needs to operate. Unless your program is really small, you'll want to put your RAM disk into extended or expanded memory, not into conventional. To create a RAM disk, you have to use a program that fools your system into believing that it has more drives than BIOS reports. DOS 5.0 comes with a utility, called RAMDRIVE.SYS, that does just this. RAMDRIVE.SYS is loaded from the CONFIG.SYS file.

Now, one option is to load RAMDRIVE.SYS into conventional memory by omitting the HIGH part of DEVICE*HIGH* in the statement. Why waste the space, though? If you have already loaded EMM386.EXE, you can install device drivers (RAMDRIVE.SYS is really a device driver) and other programs into the UMA, or the area of memory located between 640K and the 1024K mark. If you don't have space for RAMDRIVE.SYS in the UMA, DOS will load it into conventional memory by default. Here's an example of the statement that it takes to have RAMDRIVE.SYS loaded into the UMA without any command-line parameters to fine-tune the installation:

DEVICEHIGH=RAMDRIVE.SYS

The last statement makes a RAM disk of 64K. Since I have three physical drives, RAMDRIVE.SYS names the RAM disk with the next available drive letter, drive "D." Need to make your RAM disk bigger? If so, the next thing to place into the statement is how big you want your RAM disk to be. You select the RAM disk size by placing the size parameter in Ks of bytes (in our *example,* it's 2 megabytes) after the "RAMDIVE.SYS" part of the statement, like this:

DEVICEHIGH=RAMDRIVE.SYS 2048

You can also tailor the sector size. RAMDRIVE.SYS lets you do this so that you can create a RAM disk that uses space efficiently for the work you're doing. Let's say you run out of RAM disk space while working. It seems that you should have enough, but the drive keeps filling.

The default sector size made for you if you don't give a sector size parameter is 512K. If you specify a smaller sector size like 256K or 128K you may be able to get a little more room on your RAM disk. This is true because DOS will use an entire sector to store a file or data that is clearly smaller in size than the sector size, so some space is under-utilized. This setting is optional. You can specify a smaller sector size by adding the needed parameter to the statement that loads RAMDRIVE.SYS like this:

DEVICEHIGH=RAMDRIVE.SYS 2048 256

Let's say you have your memory configured as expanded memory. To tell RAMDRIVE.SYS to make you a RAM disk in expanded memory, use this statement:

DEVICEHIGH=RAMDRIVE.SYS 2048 256 /A

Setting Up a RAM Disk

If your system is configured to utilize *extended* memory, you may want to place your RAM disk in extended memory with the following statement:

DEVICEHIGH=RAMDRIVE.SYS 2048 256 /E

Making Your Programs Fly

Let's make a RAM disk and place a program on it to see just how fast a RAM disk can be. Here's the statement that I've placed in my CONFIG.SYS file to load RAMDRIVE.SYS, and make Micrografx *Designer* 3.1 fly for me from a 2 meg RAM disk placed in extended (/E) memory:

DEVICEHIGH=RAMDRIVE.SYS 2048 /E

In my AUTOEXEC.BAT file, I've also added these lines:

MKDIR D:\DESIGNER
COPY C:\WINDOWS\DESIGNER*.* D:\DESIGNER

These two lines make a directory to hold *Designer* on my RAM drive, and they then copy my program to the RAM drive. My icon properties in *Windows* call up *Designer* from D:\DESIGNER.

Don't let *Windows* tell you that you can't use a directory or file name that doesn't exist yet because you haven't made the RAM disk. Go ahead and save the properties anyway and it will work fine in the future. Just don't forget to make the drive/directory in RAM and copy the files.

Self-Erasing Junk Files

No matter how careful you are, there are some programs that insist on creating temporary work files, and then fail to delete them from the directory where they place them. Both DOS and *Windows*-based applications may make temporary files.

If you make a RAM disk with a subdirectory of \TEMP, you will never have to check for and delete these nuisance files again. You need to make a RAM disk first, then make a directory to hold the temporary files on the RAM disk. You then have to tell both

DOS and *Windows* that all programs should use the RAM disk for working with temporary files.

If you do this, your system will *run faster*, jump higher (just kidding), and will erase all temporary files every time you reboot or power-down the computer. In your CONFIG.SYS, add this line:

```
DEVICE=RAMDRIVE.SYS 1024 /E
```

This line makes a RAM disk on the next available drive letter, makes it 1 megabyte in size (*you* may need more), and places it in extended memory (optional). Now for the AUTOEXEC.BAT file:

```
MKDIR D:\TEMP
SET TEMP=D:\TEMP
SET TMP=D:\TEMP
```

Now, you only use the D: drive designation if your RAM drive is to be named D:. The drive RAMDRIVE.SYS makes for your system may have a different drive letter handed to it.

That's about it. We've made RAM disks for different reasons. We've seen programs fly compared to their normal performance on a physical hard drive. The bottom line is that you're not shackled to the performance levels of your hard drive any more. If your system will accept the additional memory, you can configure big RAM disks—*gigabytes* even, as long as you are working with *extended* memory. Even *expanded* memory users can make RAM disks of 10, 20 or even 30 megabytes. RAM disks are limited in size only by the amount of your system memory and the ultimate memory capacity ceilings of expanded and extended memory.

Take a few minutes to experiment with RAM disks and what they can do for you. Sometimes a small program that gets used often will fit on a very small RAM disk. It's up to you to figure out how *you* can use this DOS 5.0 utility to make your life move along a little bit faster—and easier.

Chapter Six
Programming in DEBUG

DEBUG is one of the great mysteries of DOS. It's curious because all the magazines and computer pundits will steer you away from DEBUG. Yet it's tantalizing because the same magazines and computer pundits will have you create DEBUG scripts that build wondrous little programs.

How can they get away with it?

As a tool, DEBUG is the ideal way to explore DOS without having to buy extra software. *DOS Secrets* touched on DEBUG in that manner. For this book, and in this chapter, we'll discuss how DEBUG can be used to program your PC. No prior programming knowledge or math skills are required for this safari.

How to Program in DEBUG

DEBUG is a multifaceted tool. It works primarily with memory; you can examine or change memory in your PC using various DEBUG commands. You can also load "raw" information from disk, in the form of files or sectors, work on them in memory, then optionally write them back out to disk.

In addition to peeking through memory, DEBUG is a programmer's tool. Those same programs you can load from disk can be taken apart by DEBUG, *disassembled* into their little pieces so a programmer can see how they work (or how they don't work, which is where DEBUG gets its name). Conversely, you can use DEBUG to put the programs back together. This process is called *assembly* and it's the *assembly language* that DEBUG uses to help you build programs.

The major drawback to all this is that DEBUG does its counting in base 16, known as *hexadecimal*. This is fine for the computer, as well as for computer programmers who use hexadecimal (hex) to keep track of their stock options. But in the real world, where humans have ten fingers, we count in base 10. This makes it confusing when you see the hex number 10—which really means 16 of something.

DEBUG is big on hexadecimal, which makes it daunting for the beginner. This chapter skirts around the issue by telling you exactly what to type. If you do any experimenting on your own, however, keep in mind that the numbers DEBUG displays are in hex—not decimal. The following table lists common conversions between hex and decimal, in case you're curious.

Decimal	Hex
1	1
2	2
3	3
4	4
5	5
6	6
7	7
8	8
9	9
10	A
11	B
12	C
13	D
14	E
15	F
16	10

Hexadecimal uses the letters A through F to represent values 10 through 15. A value of 16 is the "10" in hex.

Creating a DEBUG Program Script

Using a text editor like the EDIT program that comes with DOS 5.0, create a text file named HELLO.SCR. Place the following lines of text into that file:

Programming in DEBUG

```
E109 "Greetings from DEBUG!$"
MOV DX,109
MOV AH,9
INT 21
INT 20

RCX
1F
N HELLO.COM
W
Q
```

Note the blank line between the INT 20 and RCX. This is important. Make sure you have a blank line in there before you save the file to disk.

Back at the DOS prompt, you'll feed the above text file into DEBUG using input redirection. Type in the following:

C:\ DEBUG HELLO.SCR

Press Enter and DEBUG is fired up, but the keystrokes come from the file HELLO.SCR. If everything goes according to plan, DEBUG will soon quit and you'll have a small program file on disk, HELLO.COM. Type HELLO at the DOS prompt to see what you've created.

Examining Your Work

You could have entered the keystrokes in HELLO.SCR manually, but things work so much more smoothly with a script file. The magazines do things that way to safely insulate you from DEBUG—but there's really no need. Here is a breakdown of what the HELLO.SCR commands did in DEBUG:

E109 "Greetings from DEBUG!$"

The E command "pokes" bytes into memory. Here, you're poking a string of text into memory at location 109 hex.

Did you notice how the string ends with a dollar sign? That's the end-of-text marker for strings as far as DOS is concerned. (I know—it doesn't make sense. What would you expect?)

```
A
MOV DX,109
MOV AH,9
INT 21
INT 20
```

A is the Assemble command in DEBUG. The next four lines are assembly language instructions that tell the microprocessor to do something. MOV is the move instruction, which puts a value into the microprocessor. DX and AH are microprocessor *registers*, the places where values are stored. INT is another assembly language instruction. Two of them are used: INT 21, which tells DOS to do something (in this case, display a line of text); and INT 20, which is the instruction to "quit" and return to the DOS prompt.

Lost? Probably. This is daunting stuff. Computer programming in assembly language is the most insane of art forms. It takes real weirdos to understand what's going on, so don't be intimidated by it. Suffice it to say, you're working with your computer on a low, low level. That implies power, since you're directly plugging into the microprocessor, but also a high degree of confusion, since the microprocessor doesn't speak much English.

That group of instructions makes up the entire program. Here is how a true computer programmer would read them:

Instruction	Meaning
MOV DX,109	Put the value 109 (hex) into register DX. That value, 109, is the location of the text string poked into memory with the E command.
MOV AH,9	Put 9 into register AH. That's the code for the DOS function call "Output character string." The string of text can be anything, but must end with a dollar sign.
INT 21	This is the DOS function call routine. That means control will be passed to DOS's internals, which examine the microprocessor's AH register. When it finds a 9, it then looks to the DX register to find the string to display.

Programming in DEBUG

INT 20   This tells DOS that the program has finished. DOS takes over and displays its prompt again.

Programming DOS

Which hat was that pulled out of? Information on programming DOS can be obtained from a number of sources. Our favorite is Ray Duncan's *Advanced MS-DOS Programming* from Microsoft Press. It lists all the information about DOS function calls and microprocessor registers. It's a bit advanced, but if you're hungry for more information, that's where you should turn.

The assembly language instructions are followed by a blank line in the HELLO.SCR file. That blank line tells DEBUG to get out of the assembly mode and return to the command mode. The next few lines contain commands to DEBUG, telling it how big the file is, its name, and directing DEBUG to write the file to disk.

RCX
1F

The RCX command tells DEBUG to change the microprocessor's CX register. The new value put into CX is 1F (hex), which is the exact size of the program you've just created. (The size includes the assembly language instructions, 9 bytes, plus the string of text, 22 bytes. The file is 31 bytes long.)

N HELLO.COM

This command gives the file a name, HELLO.COM.

W

The W command directs DEBUG to write the file out to disk. The file must first be named with the N command and its size is held in the CX register.

Q

The Q command quits DEBUG, returning you to the DOS prompt.

All in all, this stuff isn't hairy. There's really no way to crash your computer or erase your hard drive here (as long as you're not careless). If you mess up with the assembly language instructions, then the program just won't work (it may lock up your computer, however). If you mess up the DEBUG instructions, you just won't create a program. There's no danger, but the thrill is still there.

Debugging the Program

To see how everything works, type the following at the DOS prompt:

C:\ DEBUG HELLO.COM

DEBUG will pop back with its hyphen prompt, ready for action. The file HELLO.COM has been loaded from disk and it's read for debugging. Type the R command at the hyphen prompt:

AX=0000 BX=0000 CX=001F DX=0000 SP=FFFE BP=0000 SI=0000 DI=0000
DS=1854 ES=1854 SS=1854 CS=1854 IP=0100 NV UP EI PL NZ NA PO NC
1854:0100 BA0901 MOV DX,0109

What you see are the microprocessor's *registers* displayed. This is all very complex and kind of interesting. But notice the bottom line: You'll see the MOV DX,109 instruction that starts your program. DEBUG has taken the program apart and is showing it to you a piece at a time.

Type the P command and press Enter. P is the *process* command and it shows you another register display. Take a look at the top line after the DX. You'll see the value 0109, which tells you that the microprocessor has "moved" 109 into the DX register. The new command at the bottom of the screen is MOV AH,9. Press P and watch the AX register on the top line.

After pressing Enter, you'll see the value 0900 in the AX register. Why 900 and not 9? Because AH is the AX "high" register. The other half is the AL or AX "low" register. When you move 9 into AH, you're only moving into the upper half of the AX register; the other half remains at zero (00).

The next instruction is INT 21. This is the instruction that calls DOS, telling it to display the text. Press P and Enter. You'll see the text displayed, then another register listing.

Press P a final time to process the INT 20 instruction. DEBUG responds with:

Program terminated normally

Congratulations, you've just "stepped" through your first program using DEBUG. Type Q and Enter to return to DOS.

The post mortem on all this is simple: You've used DEBUG to read in your program and prove that it works. When DEBUG really comes in useful is when things *don't* work. Programmers use debuggers to traipse through their code to see what went awry. They can then fix things and save it back to disk (and try, try again).

Before moving on, don't delude yourself with visions of disassembling DOS or *Windows* to see how they work. DEBUG is a simple debugger and can't handle anything too big (and can't handle EXE programs at all). For quick and dirty work, however, nothing can beat it or its price.

If you really want to DEBUG an EXE file, first rename it with a BIN extension. You can then load it into DEBUG and view it in memory with the D command. Note that EXE programs are generally too large to step through using the P command.

Chapter Seven
Using PC Graphics

One of the burning issues of the '90s will be computer graphics. This was a laughable subject on PCs up until recently. The early computers had primitive "block" graphics. Can you remember seeing ugly blocks on a screen looking like bad masonry and having a computer user enthusiastically gush that it was actually a rendering of Albert Einstein? Those days are long gone.

Though DOS is still lame when it comes to graphics, the PC is bursting with graphics potential. This chapter discusses how DOS uses graphics (which takes about four paragraphs), but also elaborates on PC graphics displays plus the various graphics file formats used by powerful graphics software under DOS.

PC Graphics Displays

Your personal computer's display generally works in two modes, text and graphics. When the monitor is working in text mode, the screen is made up of characters. These characters are found in the ASCII extended character set. The ASCII character set is made up of 256 characters, each of which can be displayed on the screen.

When your hardware is run in graphics mode, each tiny dot—or pixel—on your screen is managed separately. The pixels are small; on most monitors they are measured in millimeters. The pixel width on my monitor is .28 millimeters across—that's almost small enough to draw a happy face on the head of a pin.

When you hear people talk about the dots in the graphical sense, you'll hear the term *pixel* substituted for *dot*. Since the color, intensity, etc. is handled on a pixel-by-pixel basis as it is displayed on your monitor, it's a lot more work for your computer to work with 640 by 480 variables (pixels) than it is for it to work with 25 by 80 (characters). This single factor makes text-based programs forever faster. It's also the same reason why '286 users are not thrilled with the performance of *Windows*. There is simply not enough muscle inside the case of your computer to make *Windows* work very quickly compared to the lightning-fast text-based applications you may be used to.

Your software is either written to be run in text mode, graphics mode or a combination of text and graphics mode. Some applications do actually use both. *PC Tools* uses graphical backgrounds and screen objects and then pastes text characters onto these backgrounds and objects. In this way you get the benefit of the speed that text mode offers, with the diversity of appearance that graphics backgrounds can provide.

There are several common graphics modes that your system may be able to display. The graphics standards that we're adapting to today are ever-changing. In 1991, the standard to which everyone adapted was VGA, or 640 by 480. In 1992, with the release of *Windows* 3.1, the 800 by 600 mode of display (also called Super VGA) became popular with users of the Microsoft *Windows* graphical environment.

When you pack more pixels on your monitor, you can lose definition on each pixel. This is because the abilities of the monitor are taxed more heavily when you ask it to manage more, smaller pixels on the same screen area.

In a nutshell, the greatest benefit of higher resolution is in the number—or size—of objects that can be displayed on one monitor's screen without having to scroll in any direction just to see it all. In *Windows*, you can place more icons in the Program Manager's group windows without having to use the scroll bars to view them all. You can also run more applications in windows at the same time, and work with them all. With DOS applications like Lotus' *1-2-3* spreadsheet products, you may want to display smaller numbers on your spreadsheet to allow you to see more of the spreadsheet at any one time.

It's kind of like using a magnifying glass on a piece of paper. Imagine 640 by 480 resolution as a document on your desk being viewed with a weak magnifying glass. Then picture 800 by 600 resolution as the document being viewed without a magnifying

Using PC Graphics 63

glass. Same document, different perspective. You can actually change how DOS displays characters when you're using DOS.

Using the MODE Command

Among other things, the MODE command is used to set the video display to a particular graphics mode. If you want to use MODE, don't forget to install ANSI.SYS from your CONFIG.SYS file first. MODE uses ANSI.SYS to translate for it in some cases.

Just in case you're a little fuzzy on the status of your system's display, printing and communications devices, try running MODE from the DOS prompt just to see what mode your monitor is operating in right now. MODE will show you some important information about what your system is up to. It's best to check up on the system before you make any changes with the MODE command. Use this next statement to take a peek at the current status of your peripheral devices:

MODE /STATUS

Notice how the info scrolls across your monitor before you can read it? Better redirect MODE's output to MORE.COM so you get a chance to read it. It's just like using DIR/P to be able to read long directory listings. This is how you use MORE.COM to give yourself a break:

MODE /STATUS MORE

Remember, by using MODE, you can manipulate the monitor/card combination to be downward-compatible only if your video card is capable of doing this. *MODE or no MODE, you cannot force a monitor/card combo to be upward-compatible if it is not capable.* Don't bother to try to switch a CGA monitor into a EGA or VGA monitor's mode with the MODE command. Something else to remember: Some software works directly with your system's video card. Once you run these applications (and some environments), your mode settings may be negated by the application. You simply have to try it to find out for sure.

You can make your color monitor display monochrome characters on an 80-column screen. Just use this syntax to do so:

MODE BW80

Here's the line you should use to switch back to 80-column color graphics from a monochrome monitor:

MODE CO80

If you want to run two displays from one computer, you need to use the MODE command to tell the computer which display is primary. Sorry, you can't run two monochrome or two VGA adapters from one system and manage both with MODE.

Here's the statement to add to your AUTOEXEC.BAT file to make your monochrome monitor the primary, or active monitor:

MODE MONO

The MODE MONO command makes your monochrome monitor display 80 columns of text by default. *Sorry, but you can't change the number of columns displayed on a monochrome monitor using MODE.*

You can use MODE to tailor how many columns and rows are displayed on your screen at any one time (using a color graphics monitor) with the following command line:

MODE 40

Your choices on column width for a color graphics adapter are either 40 or 80 columns. You can change the number of lines on your display, too—*if* your display adapter supports it.

Make sure you've installed ANSI.SYS in your CONFIG.SYS file before you try to work with numbers of rows (lines) using the MODE command.

Your choices are 25, 43 and 50 lines for a VGA monitor and 25 or 43 for an EGA monitor. Try using this statement at the DOS prompt and see what you get:

MODE CON: COLS=40 LINES=50

It should look pretty funky compared to what you're used to. Now change it back by simply changing the numerical parameters to 80 columns and 25 lines. That's what you're probably used to.

You don't have to be locked into any particular mode, either. Some folks like to get more on a screen only when they use their favorite shell, for example. The character shape takes a little getting used to, but you can see more directories and files on one screen. It's kinda nice if you have a large drive and/or complicated directory structures.

You *could* make a batch file to change the monitor mode before you run your favorite shell or file manager, for example, and then switch back to standard VGA (80 by 25) after you quit the application. That way you only use the 80 by 50 mode when in your shell. Don't try this with DOSSHELL: It has its own configuration setup, and will not respond to MODE's gyrations. Name the file that switches your hardware to 80 by 50 as MODE8050.BAT. Then name the file that switches your display back to normal VGA as MODE8025.BAT. Make sure the batch files are in the same subdirectory as the file management program, or in a directory named in the PATH= statement in your AUTOEXEC.BAT file; if not, DOS won't be able to find them.

Be sure the MODE8050.BAT file contains this command:

MODE CON: LINES=50 COLS=80

This is how the command in MODE8025.BAT should look:

MODE CON: LINES=25 COLS=80

That's it! Now all you have to do is type in the name of either batch file to change your system's display mode. One batch file changes the display mode so that you see twice as many lines of data on your screen, and the other returns the screen to normal viewing. Kinda nice.

The Screen Dump

One of the more fun things about DOS at the command line is the ability to print whatever block text is on the screen by simply pressing the Print Screen key (if you have a 101-key enhanced keyboard). If you're interested in printing graphics, read on past this section to the part about GRAPHICS.COM.

I would have been a happy guy if Microsoft had kept the Print Screen feature when designing *Windows*. Oh, well. One can buy utilities that redirect screen content to the printer by assigning another key or keystroke combination.

If you have the 101-enhanced keyboard, press the Print Screen key to send the contents of your screen to your printer. If you have an 84-key keyboard, press and hold the Shift key while pressing the Print Screen key to accomplish the same thing. If you're in *Windows*, a copy of your screen will be stored in the Clipboard instead of being routed to your printer.

Printing Graphics

DOS will let you print the contents of a screen whenever you're viewing ASCII characters or text. The Shift+Print Screen keystroke combination is one of the real power surges an early DOS user can relate to. Sort of like a youngster that discovers what the doorknob is *really* for! At least that's the way it was for me. Anyway, if you want to dump the contents of a text screen (the screen you work with at the DOS prompt), you just press that handy little keystroke combination. But what if you want to print a graphics file from the DOS prompt? What to do? You can't do it from the DOS prompt. No way!

Way! Here's a cool way to print a graphics file or text the same way you're used to—directly to the printer. DOS 5.0 comes with a nice little program to do just that! It's called GRAPHICS.COM.

You run the GRAPHICS.COM program from the DOS prompt like any program; you just place the name of the graphics file at the end of the command statement. It can get a little confusing at this point, so we're going to show you the syntax to use, and let you pick the graphics file name. Just substitute your file name for our *<filename>* wherever you see it in this section.

The only other real thought process you need to consider is picking the output device for your hard copy. You need to tell GRAPHICS.COM what sort of printer you're using, because it doesn't know. And it can't check. You can pick a generic printer, like we do in the following example, or you can specify to maximize output quality and speed. By the way, GRAPHICS.COM prints in the current display mode, so if you've switched to a mode other than an 80-column screen mode, that's what you're gonna get when you use GRAPHICS.COM to print.

Printing Graphics and Text Using the Print Screen Key

If you just want to use the good old Print Screen combo keystroke to dump graphics and text screens to any old printer, you should load GRAPHICS.COM into your AUTOEXEC.BAT file so it's memory-resident when you need it. You can specify what printer you'll use, and what kind of output you need. Now, we're using the <*filename*> substitution gimmick so you know how to print a file in our examples.

If you want only to be able to print the contents of any screen, all you have to do is insert the preferred example of our syntax into your AUTOEXEC.BAT file and use the Shift-Print Screen keys to print what you want. Obviously, don't include a file name in the statement that goes into your AUTOEXEC.BAT file.

Printing Files With GRAPHICS.COM

If you want files to print in color, you need to specify which color printer you will be using. In these next examples, you need to plug in your file name instead of <*filename*>. If you're just setting up to use the Print Screen key, omit the <*filename*> in your AUTOEXEC.BAT statement.

This line prints graphics files, black on white, on any IBM-compatible printer capable of printing graphics:

GRAPHICS GRAPHICS <*filename*>

This line prints graphics files, white on black, on any IBM-compatible printer capable of printing graphics:

GRAPHICS GRAPHICS <*filename*> /R

This line prints graphics files, black on white, on any HP LaserJet II-compatible printer:

GRAPHICS LASERJETII <*filename*>

This line prints graphics files, black on white, on any HP DeskJet compatible printer:

GRAPHICS DESKJET <filename>

This line prints graphics files, black on white, on any HP PaintJet compatible printer:

GRAPHICS PAINTJET <filename>

Graphics Files Translation Utilities

Most applications that are made to work with graphics files will import or export to several popular file formats. By far, the best I've seen in this category is Micrografx *Designer* 3.1.

Here's a list of the file formats that it will import:

AI	Adobe *Illustrator*
CGM	Computer Graphics Metafile
DRW	Micrografx *Drawing*
DXF	Data Exchange Format
GEM	GEM Metafile
GRF	Micrografx Graph
PCT	Macintosh PICT file
PCX	ZSoft Image File
PIC	Micrografx Picture
TIF	Tag Image File Format
TXT	ANSI Text
WMF	*Windows* Metafile
WPG	*WordPerfect* Graphics File

Here's a list of the file formats that *Designer* 3.1 will export:

AI	Adobe *Illustrator*
CGM	Computer Graphics Metafile
DRW	Micrografx *Drawing* 3.01
DRW	Micrografx *Drawing* 2.0
DRW	Micrografx *Drawing* 1.X
DXF	Data Exchange Format
EPS	Encapsulated PostScript (with TIFF)
GEM	GEM Metafile
HP	HP Graphics Language

Using PC Graphics

PCT	Macintosh PICT file
PCX	ZSoft Image File
PIC	Micrografx Picture
PS	PostScript
TIF	Tag Image File Format
WMF	*Windows* Metafile
WPG	*WordPerfect* Graphics File

Each one of these file formats are discussed in great detail in *Designer*'s Help section. It goes to show you that application makers are taking file formats seriously these days as part of the quest for market share, or you wouldn't be seeing this caliber of file-format management in Micrografx *Designer*.

If you feel you need a program that's made to do only file conversions, and you're willing to pay about the same price to get that dedication without the technical drawing expertise of a product like *Designer*, there are two popular file-conversion utilities that are made for that purpose. One is *HotShot Graphics* by SymSoft; the other is *Zenographics Import*.

HotShot Graphics is a drawing/file format conversion/screen capture program that runs from the DOS prompt. It includes a *Windows*-based program that handles many of its tasks from within *Windows*—but it eventually requires you to do the dirty work from DOS or a DOS window.

File Format Conversion

The fact is, the makers of technical drawing packages have traditionally offered very flexible file format conversion utilities. I think it's due to their position right smack in the middle of the Tech Drawing–CAD–Graphics–Word Processing businesses. If you're thinking about spending hard cash for one of these conversion programs, consider upgrading your word processor. The so-called "executive" word processors now handle a lot more file formats than ever before, and you may kill two bills with one check by upgrading now.

HotShot Graphics has been around for quite some time, and it seems virtually bugless. The program captures to the Clipboard or a file from *Windows* (and to a file in *HotShot*'s proprietary format if the screen is captured from the DOS prompt).

HotShot Graphics converts between these popular file formats:

PCX
gray-scaled PCX
GEM IMG
MS-Paint MSP
MacPaint PNT
gray-Scaled *MacPaint* PNT
TIFF
WordPerfect WPG
Encapsulated PostScript

Screen-Capture Utilities

The best buys in screen-capture programs are: Inner Media's *Collage Plus*; Anderson Consulting and Software's *Tiffany+*; and *DoDot* by Halcyon. These three products do things somewhat differently, but they all essentially capture screens into most of the popular file formats or the *Windows* Clipboard. If you want a utility that will capture and save to most graphics file formats from both DOS and *Windows*, you'll want *Collage Plus*.

If you are capturing screens from within *Windows* only, you'll want *Tiffany+* or *DoDot*. My personal favorite is *Tiffany+* because it saves files in several file formats as well as allowing you to work with differing versions of those formats. This is really useful when you are working with someone else's graphics files. All of these programs work with some mix of the list of formats handled by Micrografx *Designer* 3.1 (listed earlier).

You can't run a *Windows* screen-capture utility until *Windows* is operational, and you can't use most text-based screen-capture utilities to capture *Windows*' graphical screens during installation. It takes a true TSR that maps the Print Screen key to another key or keystroke combination to be able to capture screen contents at virtually all times.

Redirecting keystrokes is how *Collage Plus*, a screen-capture utility from Inner Media Inc., captures screens while *Windows* is going through its own installation process. *Windows* actually switches from text to graphics mode during its installation. It also takes control of the Print Screen key in the process.

Some Parting Thoughts

If you don't have a graphics printer, and use GRAPHICS.COM to send graphical files and screens to your printer, you will probably get pages full of randomly placed ASCII characters.

- If your printer has a graphics mode, but isn't set up to run in graphics mode, you'll get the same garbage.

- Correspondingly, if you have an old dot-matrix printer that does not print the upper ASCII character set, your lines and filler characters will be substituted with "M"s, "L"s and so on—even if you don't use GRAPHICS.COM.

- If you try to send a graphics file to a printer that doesn't have enough memory to accept the file from your system in one fell swoop, you may have a long wait for the printer to print your file—the printer may not release your system to continue until it finishes printing the file.

- The printer may print as much of the file as it can accept, then form-feed to continue printing the remainder of the file. The fancier the graphics in the file, the more memory it takes to handle it. This can be a real problem with some laser printers that have only 512K of memory to work with.

All in all, the GRAPHICS.COM utility is a vast improvement over what we had to work with in previous versions of DOS. At last we can print graphics files and screen dumps to laser printers and inkjet printers and get at least an acceptable proof. What the heck! For the occasional user, it's a great way to print graphic files with limited system memory—especially if you either don't have or can't run one of the application programs with all the bells and whistles made to do the same thing.

Chapter Eight
Computer Communications

There is a whole world out there waiting to talk to you! If you're a member of InterNet or any of the other Information Services, you can talk to computers at universities around the world. You can leave messages for Carl Sagan at Cornell. You can even tell Roger Ebert (of *Siskell and Ebert*) that he was wrong about your favorite movie. You can chat openly with anyone who belongs to these services who is willing to talk with you, as long as they are also logged-on to the service at the same time you are. If they're not, you can simply leave them a message, with or without an accompanying file—all in their E-mail box.

This chapter touches upon PC communications, a highly important part of personal computing. You can chat from one computer to the next, across the office, or around the globe, providing you have the proper hardware. In addition to chatting, information and files can be exchanged as part of the larger world of "networking." This chapter un-pops the rivets and shows you how PC communications really works.

Connecting to a Modem

To communicate with other computers, you don't really have to manage at the DOS level anymore, but there are some things you should know since DOS is always there in the background.

If you're planning to use a modem with V.34, V.42 or any of the prominent compression methods, you need to configure the serial port that your modem will be using. For example, if you are using a 2400 baud Hayes-compatible modem with MNP-5, and/or V.42 compression capabilities, you will want to use the MODE command to enable your serial port to accommodate the higher transfer rates that your modem will support.

Even if your modem is only a 2400 baud unit, you need to tell DOS that the port *can* operate at a rate of up to 9600 baud when using a modem that transacts data using these newer file compression techniques. What you are really doing is enabling the modem to operate at its full rated speed using any of the recent file compression and transfer protocols. Set the serial port to 9600 baud with this command:

LOADHIGH MODE COM2:9600,N,8,1

In the case of this last statement, I'm asking DOS to:

- Place MODE into the UMA. (Why not use the dormant space?)
- Manage COM2 with this command. (My modem is set to use COM2.)
- Set the port's maximum data transfer speed in baud to 9600.
- Set the parity to none, or N. (Again, these are my modem settings.)
- Set the number of data bits to 8. (More modem settings.)
- Set the stop bits to 1. (Another modem setting.)

When you set a modem, you set four different things: the speed at which the modem talks, plus three other items collectively referred to as the *data word format*.

The modem's speed is measured in *bits per second,* or bps. This is also often referred to as a *baud rate,* though this is technically incorrect. Common speeds for modems are 300, 1200, 2400, 9600, 14K and 19.2K bps.

The data word format contains three elements: word size, parity, and the number of stop bits. Though there are numerous combinations, only two are common for PC communications: 8N1, for an 8-bit word size, no parity, and 1 stop bit; and 7E1, for a 7-bit word size, even parity, and 1 stop bit.

Your modem should now be able to perform up to its scheduled transfer rates without being constrained by the serial port. Check your modem's documentation for the correct settings to use, just

Computer Communications 75

in case the settings I've given here are not appropriate for *your* particular modem.

Calling a BBS

When calling a BBS, you in effect use a modem and communications software to emulate a terminal on the BBS's computer. You become a remote keyboard and monitor attached to the BBS via the phone line. The modem handles the translations between the computers and the phone lines. Your communications software handles the translations between you and the modem.

Using the CTTY Command

The CTTY command switches control of a system from one console to another. A console is defined as a keyboard and display unit. You can actually hook up another terminal to your personal computer with the right cabling. You cannot add a *second* working terminal in this fashion, but you can divert control of your system to an external terminal by assigning input/output control to a serial port using the CTTY command.

Not many people use CTTY like this these days; we usually opt for network software or a software/hardware bridging arrangement of some sort. In this whole process utilizing CTTY, you are actually connecting your computer to a remote computer via serial ports.

This can be a great way of using your desktop machine from your laptop at the end of a serial cable, say, in another room of your home or office. If you have gotten used to using a laptop's keyboard, this process can prevent lots of grief by saving you the pain of switching between drastically differing keyboard layouts. If you have a laptop and the appropriate serial cable, give this a try just for fun. *You'll need a terminal emulation software package on the laptop to do this.* Most communications packages like *Procomm* and *CrossTalk* will perform standard emulation functions as part of their utility.

We'll use COM2. Plug your serial cable into COM2 on your desktop PC, and then plug the other end of the cable into COM2 of your laptop machine. We chose to use COM2 because small rodents are plugged into COM1 on both machines

In our example case we use COM2—you'll have to make sure the port you specify is indeed available. Don't use AUX instead of COM2 if you have COM1 available or in use. I know other books say you can use AUX instead of naming a com port specifically, but DOS thinks the word AUX in the command is an *alias* for COM1 (if COM1 exists). If you have more than one com port, the use of AUX instead of naming the port directly will result in the redirection of your input to COM1 by default.

If you've given COM1 to a mouse or another device, you'll have problems with using the AUX alias. If you only have one COM port and that port is COM2, you can use AUX instead, as long as the port is available and is not in use. *You cannot assign AUX to COM2 unless COM1 does not exist on your system.* Be careful. It's a lot easier and cleaner to specify the com port as we have in these examples.

Plug the unattached end of the serial cable into any com port available on your laptop. If you need to, use an adapter to convert the cable's "D" connector to the smaller type of serial port jack that laptops usually have. *If you own a mouse, one of these adapters may have been included with the mouse, and if it's not in use, this adapter should work fine.*

At this point, you should have a serial cable connected between COM2 of the desktop PC and any COM2 of the laptop PC.

Now configure your port (COM2) for the 9600 baud, no parity, eight data bits and one stop bit with the MODE command added to the AUTOEXEC.BAT file in both computers. If your laptop has just the one COM port, change COM2 to COM1 in the statement.

A spot quiz. This syntax *should* look familiar:

LOADHIGH MODE COM2:9600,N,8,1

If you're running the last command line without adding it to your AUTOEXEC.BAT file, don't reboot the machines. If you've updated and saved your AUTOEXEC.BAT file(s) with this command, reboot *both* machines. If you're not planning to do this often, you could just run the command line from the DOS prompt of each machine without having to reboot at all. The batch file additions just make it easier on a repetitive basis.

Start the terminal emulation program on your laptop, and tell it to use the COM port that you've selected on your laptop.

Now, at your desktop machine, use this command at the DOS prompt:

CTTY COM2

Your display and keyboard should seem frozen on your desktop machine, because they are. You've just bypassed these two devices electronically with the last command. Don't panic during this process. Just reboot the desktop machine and control will return to your display and keyboard.

From within your laptop's emulation program, try doing a directory. You should see the files and directories on your desktop machine. If you do, you're all set. You now have the use of your desktop machine from your remote laptop. To return control to your desktop monitor and keyboard from your laptop, use this command at the DOS prompt:

CTTY CON

That's it. Remember, if your emulation program gives you a hard time and you want to abort, retry or fail, just reboot the desktop machine. You can reverse the process, of course. There is no reason why you cannot access your laptop from your desktop machine by running CTTY on the laptop and the emulation package on the desktop machine.

Using CTTY for Security

If you run large batch files on a public system as part of a procedure or system maintenance process, you may not want anyone to be able to interrupt or even see what is transpiring during, for example, a file backup operation.

You can use the CTTY command to turn off the keyboard and the display while you run a large batch file. This could be really handy when you are doing sensitive chores on a public machine, like, say, your company's weekly payroll. These next statements (really a short batch file) will turn off the keyboard and display *and then* return control of the computer to the keyboard and display:

```
@ECHO OFF
CTTY NUL
<COMMAND LIST OR PROGRAM NAME>
CTTY CON
```

This batch file seems to *stun* your system while it runs a program or a list of DOS commands and then returns the computer to its normal state by returning control to the console (keyboard and monitor) when it's through.

What's Out There

There are lots of software packages that are made to set up your computers as a remote PC and a server. As the laptop and notebook industries price-down and ramp-up their production, solutions much more elegant than CTTY will begin to sprout like *weeds* in your computer magazines. They won't be as cheap as using CTTY, but they'll give you much more control and may even work more efficiently. The fact is, many of these programs work at the machine or hardware level and bypass DOS completely, making them faster for the user once you set them up on your machines.

For the not so faint-of-heart with the checkbook, there are programs that come with cables made to link two machines so you can transfer files between them. You can even call your desktop machine at the office from your laptop. These programs allow you complete access to the drives and devices in each computer from either machine. The phone companies must be eating this up!

Lastly, for the serious sharing tasks, popular products that network just two machines as a starter kit are not available for less than 500 dollars. Artisoft's *Lantastic* product is becoming a new standard for those who want to start *small* by networking two computers. With *Lantastic*, you don't have to pay for a 6- or 600-user network if you only have two or more machines. These starter kits contain everything you need to get rolling: software, interface cards and cabling.

Lantastic and other networking products even have graphical interfaces for Microsoft *Windows*. It doesn't get much easier.

I like to recommend *Lantastic* because I use it at home on my machines, and it was incredibly simple to install. If you can handle installing a modem, you'll have no problem with *Lantastic* or many of the other outstanding networking solutions. Now all I need is a way to network my TVs at home so I can monitor what my kids are watching from my computer!

Chapter Nine
Using Your Printer

Many people's sole use for a computer is for the creation of hard copy of one form or another. That hard copy is something on paper—a translation of a computer's electronic thoughts into a physical thing you can hold. DOS 5.0 includes several utilitarian features that can make your DOS command-line tasks much easier.

This chapter is dedicated to making DOS 5.0 handle your printing workload. Though there are thousands of different PCs available, DOS can work with a great majority. If not, then there are a number of other tricks you can teach your printer using plain old DOS, no learner's permit required.

Printing From DOS

You can print directly from the DOS prompt if you redirect the output of various DOS commands to your printer. Redirection means placing a symbol between a DOS command and a device or file name to tell DOS to send what the first command denotes to the device or file.

Normally when you do a DIR, you see the contents of your current directory on the screen. Here's how you would send to your printer what would normally display on your screen:

DIR PRN

You can substitute any LPT port if you'd like. Like AUX, using PRN as an output alias directs that output to the first of the ports of the type—LPT1 if you specify PRN—which may or may not be correct. It's better to be port-specific if you can, like this:

DIR LPT2

You can also do what many people call "printing to a file." You simply re-direct the output of your DOS commands to a file instead of the screen or a printer:

DIR <filename>

Just use *your* preferred file name instead of our <filename> syntax.

If you want to add text to the end of an existing text file, so you can place the contents of two directories in a text file for comparison, you would use this syntax to print the second DIR to an existing file:

DIR >> <filename>

The double ">>" symbol means to send the output of the command to a file, and if the file name already exists, to add the output to the end of the text in the existing file. This can be a handy little tool to use when a tech support person wants you to fax them a directory of interest so they can help you out of a fix. I use the command to print to a file and then fax the file directly through the fax/modem card in my machine. It's also a nice way to be able to store a DIR for later printing using the PRINT.EXE utility that we'll talk about later in this chapter.

At this point, I hope your brain is a maelstrom of ideas on how you can make sweet combos of DOS commands to enhance printing from the DOS prompt. If you're not really intrigued by this concept, you may be up for using DOS's PRINT.EXE utility, detailed later in this chapter.

Any way you choose, you *can* get your displayed data, file contents and combinations of them to your printer without the help of fancy-shmancy programs for which you have to pay extra. It will also help to make a DOS guru out of you.

DOS Printer Setup

If your printer is IBM- or Epson-compatible, DOS can help you create better-looking output *without* a word processor to handle the printing process. Using the MODE command, you can set your parallel ports to accommodate a few of your printing requirements.

Using Your Printer

You can set the width of printed text as well as determine how many lines will be printed. This is how you would set a printer connected to LPT1 to print text 80 characters wide for 66 lines before starting another page:

    MODE LPT1:80,6

The MODE command only allows you to set the lines-per-inch to either 6 or 8. You can set the width in columns to either 80 or 132. This last command line would be handy if you were running a 132-column printer with a perf at the 80 column mark. Many people use this type of fan fold so they don't have to change paper when they switch between printing letters and wide spreadsheets.

If your printer were set up to print 132-column spreadsheets, and you would like it to print 80-column text, this is one way to do so without physically going to the printer and resetting it with its own panel switches.

To make changes to some older printers means that settings must be made at the printer with its DIP switches. These machines make this last command line very valuable indeed!

You can make a few additional statements to your printer by including one or more of the command-line switches provided by DOS 5.0. If you want to tell DOS to keep trying to send a file to a shared printer until *your* work is done, then you would use this command:

    MODE LPT1: RETRY=R

The RETRY=R option tells DOS to assume the printer is always "ready," even though it may be printing something else.

Printing With DOS

DOS 5.0 comes with a pretty good print spooler utility. PRINT.EXE will print to a local printer only. In other words, it does not work on a network printer. PRINT.EXE does, however, work completely in the background. You can send any number of files to your print spooler (PRINT.EXE) and go on to something else while they print.

If you have only one printer and it's hooked-up to LPT1 (for example), set up the spooler before you need it by using this command statement. This would also be a good statement to place in your AUTOEXEC.BAT file if you use PRINT.EXE with any frequency:

PRINT /D:LPT1

To send the first file to your spooler, use this command:

PRINT <filename>

To *add* a file to the print queue, use this statement:

PRINT /P <filename>

If you want to send two or more files to your printer via your spooler, use this statement:

PRINT <filename> <filename> <filename> <filename>

If you want several files to print in the order that their names appear in the command line, use the /P switch like this:

PRINT /P <filename> <filename> <filename>

Should you feel the need to send all of the files in a subdirectory to the printer via the spooler, you would phrase the command:

PRINT *.*

That last one was pretty tricky, eh? That's one of the great things about PRINT.EXE. It's elegantly simple.

You can also interrupt a process or kill it completely if you need to. You can delete selective files from the print queue by using the /C command-line switch just before the single or multiple file names on a command-line statement. This command-line length cannot exceed 64 characters:

PRINT /C <filename> <filename> <filename>

This one is brutal. If you've sent files to PRINT's queue and you'd like to see what you have in the lineup, use this syntax:

PRINT

Using Your Printer

And finally, if you want to dump (delete) everything in the buffer use this command-line statement:

PRINT /T

Sorry, you can't remove PRINT.EXE from memory unless you reboot the computer.

Printer Control in the Editor

DOS 5.0 comes with a text editor that can be pretty handy if you just want to make or edit a batch file without loading a full-blown word processor. To print any file that can be read by Editor, first open the file, then select the Print option from the File menu. The figure below shows you where the Print option appears on the File menu.

Figure 9.2 illustrates that you can choose to print just the selected text or the entire document.

DOS 5.0's Editor will only print to LPT1. The Editor doesn't print well, which is why it's a text editor and not a full blown word processor. But you can weasel in some fancy printing using the special Ctrl-P command.

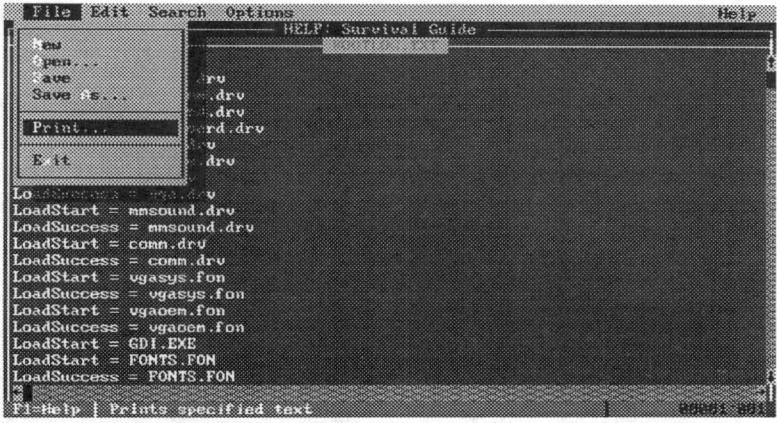

Figure 9.1: The Print options from the File menu.

Using Your Printer

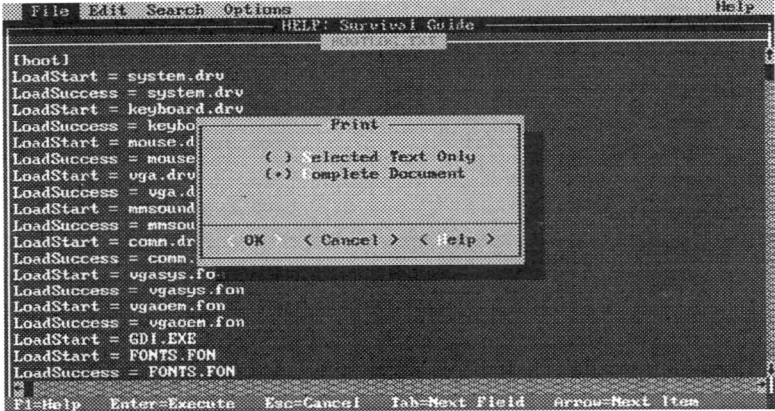

Figure 9.2: The Print dialog box.

In Ctrl-P the P stands for *Prefix*. This key allows you to insert any character into your document literally. For example, to insert the escape character you type Ctrl-P, Esc. That puts the left-pointing arrow (the symbol for the escape character) into your document. It also makes working with ANSI commands easier (see Chapter Two). For your printer, you can use Ctrl-P to insert some special printer codes.

As an example, type the following line into the Editor; type Ctrl-P, Esc when you see the ¬ character:

This is an example of ¬-1 underline ¬ -0 printing.

Above, you're entering the IBM/Epson command for underline on and underline off into the text. Print the document in the Editor and, providing your printer is IBM/Epson compatible, you'll see the work underlined.

> The command is escape-hyphen-1 for "underline on," and escape-hyphen-0 for "underline off." Other text-formatting commands are listed in your Espon or IBM printer manual.

Another handy trick is to insert the Ctrl-L character to force a new page—and to eject a page from your laser printer. This character looks like the Egyptian Ankh symbol and it's produced by typing Ctrl-P, Ctrl-L.

The Ctrl-P, Ctrl-L key combination is a great one to stick at the end of your text in the Editor. This allows the full page to be ejected from your printer.

Other handy key combinations exist, as well. Refer to your printer manual if you want to get fancy. But keep in mind that modern word processing software is much more efficient in printing fancy text. And it takes less time than manually typing in codes in the Editor.

Chapter Ten
Hard Drive Lessons

There are probably more books on managing hard drives than all other types of books put together. It seems silly, but because the hard drive is a mechanical device, there are a lot of variables. And believe me, there are a lot of different hard drives out there. That's why it's important to think hard drive *strategy* before you get to other levels of detail.

There are a lot of things you can do to enhance file management performance. Many of these *things* are simply common sense. With a little understanding, you can make your computing machine complete its tasks with less work, making it faster. This chapter contains a few simple lessons on how to keep your hard drive in order. The rest is maintenance.

Thought Processes

Once you're locked into a particular hard drive or drives, the rest of the game is what you do with them. Here are some basic rules of thumb:

- The more files on the drive, the slower it will be. Don't place needless files on your hard drive to begin with. When you load it up and then delete files on a frequent basis, you create fragmentation that slows your drive. You will also need to compact your drive more often.

- Run CHKDSK/F at least once a week. CHKDSK converts lost clusters into files that you can review. It creates the files in your root directory with a file-name extension of CHK. Get a text editor that can read the files that CHKDSK converts to CHK files in your root directory. If the files are unrecognizable garble (binary), then you have probably lost an executable file to fragmentation, and one of your applications is not going to run properly. If you review the contents of a CHKDSK file and you recognize some of the information as being part of a data file, you will need to copy the backup version from your floppies back to your hard drive, because the part of the CHK file you are reviewing will be missing from your original data file when you try to use it. Running CHKDSK/F is a requisite before you use any disk-compaction utility.

- Get a disk-compaction utility and *use it weekly*. It doesn't matter how much you *think* you need it. Do it weekly anyway. Most competent, popular, disk-compaction utilities will perform several diagnostic routines during the compaction process. If you have any media defects that are recent, the utility will notify you. The sooner you know about media defects on your hard drive, the better. It's a lot easier to let one of these utilities find and exclude media defects before you try to load another program on your hard drive—and it fails to run properly.

- Always use SMARTDrive or another good hard disk caching program. Be sure to use version 4.0 or higher of SMARTDrive, if possible. These versions have many more features, like sensing when you've pressed Ctrl-Alt-Del. In this event, SMART-Drive 4.0 does not allow the machine to reboot until all data stored in SMARTDrive's cache has been updated to the hard drive. You'll see a message asking you to wait while SMART-Drive stalls the reboot to save your data.

- If your hard drive has an on-board cache, as many modern drives do, measure the drive's performance with a software disk-caching program like SMARTDrive and then measure the drive's performance without the software cache. You should find that disk-caching software will improve performance in all but the most unusual circumstances.

- If your hard drive has an on-board cache, don't upgrade your controller just to gain an additional hardware cache. Many controllers were made during the first two years of the IDE revolution that sported on-board caches of 32K or 64K. Some had

Hard Drive Lessons

caches of even more RAM. The concept was great when drives did not have built-in caches. If you tend to work with files that are smaller in size than the drive's hard cache size, you won't gain much of a benefit by upgrading to a controller with a cache of 1 megabyte or more. If your drive is cached and you are using a cached IDE controller, you may actually experience a *delay* in transacting data because you have involved two sets of caching hardware that must be located in the data path.

- If you must keep little-used files on your hard drive for whatever reason, use a file-compression utility to make the files as small as possible. If you tend to end up with a lot of graphic files, for example, a disk-compression utility like PKZIP from PKWARE may compress the file into 10 percent of its original size without any damage to the file. You can even make each file self-expanding so you can retrieve it without the aid of the file compression utility. Of course, it makes more sense to store little-used files *in compressed format* on floppies to reclaim hard drive space.

Directory Ordering for Speed

Back when your drive was young, when it was relatively free of files, your drive whipped through its tasks. Now, it has probably slowed a bit. If you tend to access your hard drive a lot in the normal course of your work, you should think about ordering your directories so that the drive finds your frequently used application programs a little sooner.

You can order your directories so that your system finds your files faster. Directory and file ordering is simply arranging files and directories on your hard drive so that the most frequently used files (along with the files they work with) are located as close together as possible. For example, if you tend to use your *WordPerfect* application almost exclusively, you should tell your disk-compaction utility to order your directories and files so that they are located as close together on your hard drive as possible.

There are essentially three ways in which to order your files and directories:

1. Order them alpha-numerically. This is the best sort of ordering if you have no reason to order otherwise.
2. Arrange them in the order of their use by task. Simply place your oft-used directories first, second, etc.
3. Organize your files so that all your programs are located first and together. You can actually specify whether you want files with the filename extension of EXE, COM, etc. close together on your drive. This can be very effective if you tend to work with very few document or work files at one time, but you use several programs at once. *This is especially useful if you work with few data files at one time and you keep data files on floppies. Windows* multitaskers will also find this method a boon to productivity.

The real benefit to ordering is that the hardware mechanisms on your hard drive only have to go a minimal amount of distance across platters to get to the data you want. Think of the process as being like a phonograph record on a turntable. If you tend to play the same songs over and over again, you use the tone arm to place the needle at the beginning of the same old songs, even if the songs are on opposite sides of the record. Don't try to tell me you don't remember doing this in high school! You don't even want to hear those "other" tunes, so you manually place the needle just before your favorite tunes by using your hand to manipulate the tone arm. When you use the same programs and files over and over again (like spreadsheets), you ask your hard drive to do virtually the same thing you did with the record! Your hard drive will do it a lot faster, but it will still waste time needlessly. That's why we order our files. It saves a lot of time and boosts productivity.

The only problem with ordering your directories and files is that DOS doesn't do it. Instead, you need a special third-party utility. Most disk-compaction utilities will provide you with the option to order your directories during compaction. The options you have really depend on the disk-compaction software you buy.

We can suggest a few of the premier disk compaction utilities:

- *The Norton Utilities* by Symantec
- *PCTools* by Central Point Software
- *The Mace Utilities* by Fifth Generation Systems

Unfortunately, when you use an on-the-fly disk-compression program (like STAC Electronics' *Stacker*, for example) to gain space on your hard drive, you need to use the compression program's own disk compaction utility to compact or compress your drive. *Some of these disk-compaction products do not offer ordering options.*

Easy Housekeeping

To make your life easier, you can make a directory on a RAM disk called TEMP. When you copy files from a BBS, or when you copy files from a floppy and uncompress or expand them, you could do it in your TEMP subdirectory. Many folks use a *temporary or holding* directory to compress several files into one archived, compressed file. It's a good idea to place all files that need to be compressed or expanded into this TEMP directory so that you don't overwrite any files that may have the same file name (like README.TXT) in any other directory. You can inadvertently overwrite valuable files unless you segregate all of your volatile compressed files before expanding them.

When you create this TEMP directory on a RAM disk, DOS and *Windows* applications can store their temporary work files there if you tell them to do so when your AUTOEXEC.BAT file is executed. First, you create a 512K RAM disk from your CONFIG.SYS file with this statement:

```
DEVICEHIGH=RAMDRIVE.SYS 512 /E
```

Then, you include this statement in your AUTOEXEC.BAT file to make your TEMP directory on the RAM disk:

```
MKDIR E:\TEMP
SET TEMP=E:\TEMP
SET TMP=E:\TEMP
```

Each time you turn your machine off (or reboot), this RAM disk goes into the great beyond together with any files that were left on it. It's a slick way to keep your applications from trashing your directories with temporary files just because the programs were written in a sloppy fashion. If you can spare the memory, make a 512K or 1,024K RAM disk and organize it in this fashion to save yourself the clutter and the added cleanup hassles. If you multitask, make a RAM disk larger than 1 megabyte.

Backing Up Your Files

Keeping your files backed up is a major part of managing your hard disk. DOS 5.0 comes with an easy-to-use utility designed just for that purpose. With BACKUP.EXE, you can back up both files *and* directories. The overview of the process is simple: You use BACKUP.EXE to create *archival* copies of your files, and you render them usable again with DOS's RESTORE.EXE.

BACKUP.EXE converts files into a special format (archive) intended for storing your files. You can't work directly with archive files created with BACKUP.EXE. But then, it's only supposed to create files intended for storage. By the way, you can create backup copies of your data and store them in either a subdirectory on a hard drive (as long as it's not on the originating hard drive) or in the root directory of a floppy disk or disks.

You can select files for archiving based on four criteria:

- Path Name
- File Name
- Date Stamp
- Time Stamp

When you run BACKUP.EXE without specifying a target hard drive, the program asks you to specify. If you specify just the drive letter, BACKUP.EXE makes a subdirectory on the target drive called "\BACKUP," and your backup files get stored there.

Let's start in the root directory of our boot drive for our examples. This is the simplest form of the use of BACKUP.EXE from the DOS prompt:

Hard Drive Lessons

BACKUP *.* D:

This is what you might see on your machine:

C:\ BACKUP *.* D:

WARNING! FILES IN THE TARGET DRIVE
D:\BACKUP DIRECTORY WILL BE ERASED
PRESS ANY KEY TO CONTINUE . . .
*** BACKING UP FILES TO DRIVE D: ***
\CONFIG.SYS
\MIRORSAV.FIL
\AUTOEXEC.BAT
\MIRROR.FIL
\EMM386.EXE
\HIMEM.SYS
\MOUSE.SYS
\RAMDRIVE.SYS
\SMARTDRV.EXE
\SMARTDRV.SYS
\PCTRACKR.DEL
\WINA20.386
\ANSI.SYS

BACKUP.EXE copied everything it found in the root directory to the D:\BACKUP directory. Did you notice that BACKUP.EXE erases everything in the target directory when it archives? Let's backup everything to a floppy for the heck of it:

BACKUP *.* B:

This is what you might expect to see:

INSERT BACKUP DISKETTE 01 IN DRIVE B:
WARNING! FILES IN THE TARGET DRIVE
B:\ ROOT DIRECTORY WILL BE ERASED
PRESS ANY KEY TO CONTINUE . . .
*** BACKING UP FILES TO DRIVE B: ***
DISKETTE NUMBER: 01
\CONFIG.SYS
\MIRORSAV.FIL
\AUTOEXEC.BAT

```
\MIRROR.FIL
\EMM386.EXE
\HIMEM.SYS
\MOUSE.SYS
\RAMDRIVE.SYS
\SMARTDRV.EXE
\SMARTDRV.SYS
\PCTRACKR.DEL
\WINA20.386
\ANSI.SYS
```

BACKUP.EXE will copy everything it finds in the source directory or drive unless it runs out of space on the target floppy. If you look at the previous example, you'll note the Diskette Number: 01 statement just before the file listing. BACKUP.EXE keeps track of the diskettes it uses and will prompt you to insert another target diskette if you run out of diskette space.

Sooner or later, you'll probably use multiple diskettes. If BACKUP.EXE fills up the first diskette, it will ask you to insert another diskette in this fashion:

```
INSERT BACKUP DISKETTE 02 IN DRIVE B:
WARNING! FILES IN THE TARGET DRIVE
B:\ ROOT DIRECTORY WILL BE ERASED
PRESS ANY KEY TO CONTINUE . . .
*** BACKING UP FILES TO DRIVE B: ***
DISKETTE NUMBER: 02
```

BACKUP.EXE labels the target diskette with a volume name. Let's use DOS's Volume (VOL) command to see what the target diskette label looks like. Since we just used a *second* diskette in our backup process, our volume name looks like this:

```
B:\ VOL
VOLUME IN DRIVE B IS BACKUP 002
```

This disk labeling feature makes it a lot less confusing when you're restoring your backed-up floppies to your hard drive. It's always a good idea to label to your target diskettes for safety's sake.

If you want to back up all of the files in a directory as well as all of the files in the subdirectories that report to the directory, use this statement to do so:

BACKUP *.* B: /S

If you want to back up all directories and/or subdirectories to another hard drive or floppy diskette(s), run this last command from the *root* directory.

If you'd like BACKUP.EXE to make a log file containing a list of the files in the archive, use this command-line switch after the target drive designation:

/L

If you want to keep your backup archive files up-to-date but don't want to have to back up *all* of your files on a daily basis, use the next command-line switch after the target drive designation:

/M

The /M switch forces BACKUP.EXE to update an archive file on a target disk or diskette with *only* the files that have been modified since the last backup. You can also add files to an existing archive by using this next command-line switch:

BACKUP *.* B: /A

If you have only unformatted diskettes at your disposal, you can have BACKUP.EXE and FORMAT.COM format them for you as they make your backup archive files on the diskette(s). You must be certain to provide DOS with a path to both files by including the directory name for both files in the PATH= statement in your AUTOEXEC.BAT file—or by switching to your DOS directory and typing the full path name of the directories or and/or files that you are backing up. (Another good reason to put your DOS directory in your PATH= statement.) Once you get this detail cared for, you can proceed with using unformatted diskettes during your backup process by using the /F switch like this:

BACKUP *.* B: /F

This command will back up all (*.*) files in the current directory with a modification date of 10-05-91:

BACKUP *.* B: /D:10-05-91

Of course, substitute any wildcards you want if you'd like to archive only certain file types. This next command is a great way to archive all of your *Word* for *Windows* document files that have been modified since the last backup, while skipping all of the other files on an entire hard drive:

BACKUP C:*.DOC B: /M /S

Using the C:\ *.DOC part of the statement tells BACKUP.EXE to start at the top of drive C, and to only consider files with a file-name extension of DOC. The B: segment is the target drive specifier. The /M switch constrains BACKUP.EXE to looking at only modified files, and the /S switch tells BACKUP.EXE to search the entire drive for files that meet these conditions (since we invoked the command from the root directory of the source drive).

When DOS saves a file, it stamps the file with the time the file was saved as well as the date saved. This allows you to back up files by time, too, with this syntax:

BACKUP *.* B: /T:12:00:00

We chose to use noon as the time in the previous example, but you can use whatever time appeals to you. Remember, you need to use all eight characters of DOS's idea of a time stamp or you will get an error message. It also helps if you make sure your system clock is running and the time/date is set correctly.

If you're concerned about the accuracy of the time on your PC and you have a modem installed, you can find a freeware program on most BBSs that works like a macro to dial the Naval Observatory, retrieve the correct time and update your system clock without any interaction by you other than running the file. Look for a file name like NAVOBS.EXE or some variation. Variations on this theme appear on most billboards, so you won't have to look far.

Taking It Seriously

Without your hard drive, you're out of luck. Taking the time to maintain and optimize your hard drive and the data you work with is a big part of keeping your system running at its best for a long time to come. Now, it may be true that you have never worked with any of the information in this chapter before, and your PC seems to work just fine. It's sort of like thinking that you can't get a flat tire *because you've never had one.*

Don't be caught unprepared when disastrous circumstances prevail. Just follow the few simple guidelines in this chapter, like running CHKDSK, optimizing your hard drive weekly and making backups of your critical data, and you'll be ahead of the game should disaster strike. Remember, victims always say, "I thought these things only happened to other people!"

Chapter Eleven
Mondo Batch Files

Batch files are one of the saving graces of DOS. You can automate virtually any process with great results. The really cool part is, if you know DOS you know batch files. All batch files are is a collection—or batch, if you will—of DOS commands. Stick them all into a text file, name it with a BAT file-name extension and, voilà, you have a batch file. It's that easy, and it makes using DOS easier.

This chapter shows you 10 of our all-time favorite batch files. Copy these down in your editor and save them to disk in a BATCH subdirectory. They will make life a lot easier when you're working at the DOS prompt.

Formatting Disks

Formatting diskettes is one of the first things you learn when using a personal computer. DOS will format a diskette at the rated capacity of the drive you designate, unless you tell DOS otherwise in the same statement you use to format the diskette. You use the FORMAT.COM utility included with DOS 5.0 to format all of your diskettes and your hard drive(s).

Since most of us find the need to format double-sided, double-density diskettes in our high-density drives, here's a batch file called FORM720.BAT that will format a double-density 720K 3 ½-inch diskette in a 1.44 megabyte, high-density drive. Make sure the drive designation (in this case, B:) matches your system's drive address. You can use this batch file:

```
ECHO OFF
FORMAT B:/F:720
```

This simple batch file formats 5 ¼-inch 360K diskettes in a 1.2 megabyte, high-density drive:

```
ECHO OFF
FORMAT A:/F:360
```

Essentially, these two commands format low-capacity disks in high-capacity drives. If you already have low-capacity drives, DOS knows this and you don't need to specify the /F switch. If you have high-capacity drives, the only time you need to do this is when you buy low-capacity disks. And the only reason to buy low-capacity disks is if you need to send a disk to someone who has only a low-capacity drive. (Whew!)

> Always buy diskettes for the highest capacity of your drive. If you have high-capacity drives—and odds are pretty good that you do—buy only high-capacity disks. Sure, they cost more. But you'll never have to mess with the FORMAT command again.

Moving Files

DOS doesn't provide us with a utility to be used from the DOS prompt just to move files. That's why you need to create what some programmers call a "work-around." Our work-around solution is in the form of a batch file to get the job done. The file name is called MOVE.BAT. Striking, eh? Easy to recall.

This batch file *moves* only DOC files from the floppy in your A: drive to the C:\DOCS directory on a hard drive. It also deletes the files on the floppy with a file-name extension of DOC without you having to answer the "Delete all Files? (Y/N)" question. Use your favorite text editor or DOS 5.0's EDIT.COM to make this batch file.

When you're done, save the filename as MOVE.BAT. These next commands should appear in MOVE.BAT:

```
C:\DOCS
XCOPY A:*.DOC
ECHO YDEL A:\*.DOC
```

That's all there is. You can change the names of the files, drives or wildcard specification to suit your needs, but the batch file does the job.

Backup Checking

Here is a single-line batch file for *Windows* users that helps you do backups of *all* of your crucial INI files using DOS 5.0's BACKUP utility. The batch file believes that all *Windows* programs are located in subdirectories attached to your \WINDOWS directory. Save this batch file with the name of INIBACK.BAT.

The batch file checks to see if you've made any changes to INI files since the last backup using DOS's IF function (IF performs commands based on conditional statements), and only performs a backup of *changed* INI files to drive B:

```
ECHO OFF
BACKUP C:\WINDOWS\*.INI B: /M /S
IF ERRORLEVEL 4 GOTO HOSED
IF ERRORLEVEL 3 GOTO QUIT
IF ERRORLEVEL 2 GOTO SHARE
IF ERRORLEVEL 1 GOTO NONE
IF ERRORLEVEL 0 GOTO OK
:HOSED
ECHO SOMETHING WENT VERY WRONG WITH THE BACKUP!!
GOTO EXIT
:QUIT
ECHO YOU PRESSED CTRL+C ... BACKUP CANCELLED!
GOTO EXIT
:SHARE
ECHO A FILE SHARING PROBLEM PREVENTED A PERFECT BACKUP!!
GOTO EXIT
:NONE
ECHO THERE WERE NO FILES THAT NEEDED BACKUP!!
GOTO EXIT
:OK
ECHO BACKUP COMPLETED!! LOOKING GOOD!
GOTO EXIT
:EXIT
```

When you run the batch file for the first time, you'll see a list of all of your INI files as they are being archived to drive B:. Here's what happens when the batch file executes:

1. BACKUP.EXE reads the size, time and date stamp of the first file that meets its search criteria. In this case, we specified INI files only. BACKUP.EXE ignores all other files.

2. BACKUP.EXE checks the source files it finds to determine if they have been backed up recently, or if a file doesn't exist on the target drive, the /M switch causes BACKUP.EXE to back up the file.

3. The /S switch forces BACKUP.EXE to look at all files in every directory and subdirectory that report to the current directory.

4. When BACKUP.EXE considers each file that matches the file specification criteria, it returns or posts a message code. This message code or *exit code* is found in the table below:

Code	What It Means
0	This file backup completed.
1	No files needed to be backed up.
2	File-sharing conflicts caused backup failure.
3	The user pressed the Ctrl+C keys to quit.
4	Another problem caused the process to halt prematurely.

5. This is where an error-level command comes in. Error level is a condition. In the batch file, the second line reads like this:

IF ERRORLEVEL 4 GOTO HOSED

The previous line of syntax translates like this:

If the backup program posts a message *(exit code 0...4)*, go to *(goto)* the line in the batch file that begins with the colon *(:)* and word *(hosed ...etc.)* assigned to that message code, and execute that line.

In the case of the existence of the first condition, or exit code 4, DOS goes to the line that begins with :HOSED, and executes the next three lines:

```
:HOSED
ECHO Something went terribly wrong with the backup!!
GOTO EXIT
```

6. DOS says the message that you instructed it to say in the event one of the conditions in the table above exists (in the case of our example, exit code 0), and then looks for and executes (GOTO) the line that begins with :EXIT

Let's briefly look at another conditional use of *errorlevel*. If you failed to place a diskette in drive B:, you will get the good-ol' DOS error message: Abort, Retry, Fail?. If you select Fail, the message will continue to appear. If you select Retry the message will continue to appear. *I hope they fix this redundancy in the next DOS upgrade!* If you select Abort, BACKUP.EXE will return the exit code "3". DOS will interpret your choice as being the same as the error level 3 message (which is the equivalent of an abort or hitting Ctrl+C).

Because of this event, your batch file will translate this exit code by virtue of the error-level function and the value of the exit code, and will display the string that you said you wanted to see in the event this particular code was returned. That string was:

```
ECHO You pressed Ctrl+C ... Backup Cancelled!
```

You can play games with this batch file and test the use of each exit code. By the way, :EXIT doesn't really do anything but cause the end of batch file execution. It's the appropriate last line in the batch file. The line is executed and control of the DOS prompt is returned to COMMAND.COM. What *you* then see is your normal DOS prompt. The operation is complete.

An AUTOEXEC.BAT Menu

This is an example of how you can make a menu for your system using batch files. You can make these batch files with DOS's EDIT.COM. Just copy the syntax to a new file opened from EDIT and save the files as the file names given here for each batch file.

This first batch file presents a menu to do three things:

1. Runs a batch file (BAT.1) that opens your favorite word processor
2. Runs a batch file (BAT.2) that performs a backup of your critical system files
3. Runs a batch file (BAT.3) that exits to a DOS prompt so you can issue other DOS commands, and then return to the menu

Here is the first batch file, called MENU.BAT. It accepts input from you in order to execute the other three batch files:

```
ECHO OFF
CLS
ECHO.
ECHO.
ECHO.
ECHO.
ECHO.
ECHO           -MY MAIN MENU-
ECHO.
ECHO.
ECHO.
ECHO.
ECHO           1. RUN MY FAVORITE WORD PROCESSOR
ECHO.
ECHO           2. BACK UP MY SYSTEM FILES
ECHO.
ECHO.
ECHO           3. GO TO THE DOS PROMPT
ECHO.
PROMPT ENTER YOUR SELECTION
```

In order to execute any of the numbered selections, you need to create a batch file to take care of each menu selection. Let's start with the batch file that runs your word processor, in this particular example, Microsoft *Word*. Again, use EDIT.COM or your favorite ASCII text editor to make this batch file, and save it under the name 1.BAT.

Here are the contents of 1.BAT:

```
ECHO OFF
CLS
CD\WORD
PROMPT $P $G
WORD.EXE
CD\
MENU
```

1.BAT clears the screen, changes the current directory to the one where the word processor (WORD.EXE) resides, changes the prompt back to what you would expect to see and then runs the word processor. When you leave the word processor, you go back to the menu.

2.BAT will clear the screen, change directories to make your root current and run DOS's BACKUP.EXE (if it's in the PATH) to back up only the files in your root directory to drive A: Again, use a text editor to create and save 2.BAT.

Here are the contents of 2.BAT:

```
@ECHO OFF
CLS
C;
CD\
BACKUP * * A:
CD\
MENU
```

3.BAT is the batch file run when you type the number "3" at the menu. 3.BAT will place you at a DOS prompt so you can run DOS commands. The menu's prompt statement is replaced with a standard DOS prompt. In effect, another copy of COMMAND.COM is run to accomplish this. The user is told that he or she must type the word "Exit" to return to the menu screen. This manipulation of DOS makes it appear as if the MENU.BAT is a real shell program indeed. Once again, use a text editor to make this batch file, and save it as 3.BAT.

Here are the contents of 3.BAT:

```
CLS
P $G
ECHO TYPE "EXIT" TO RETURN TO MY MENU ...
COMMAND
MENU
```

3.BAT clears the screen, turns off the display of the rest of the commands in this batch file, and sets the prompt message to the standard one recommended by Microsoft. The standard prompt message indicates the current drive, followed by the directory name, then a space, and then the ">" symbol. The flashing prompt will appear immediately to the right of this symbol. You then see a message of instruction reminding you to type "EXIT" to leave the DOS prompt and return to the menu.

Batch files can be the next best thing to writing your own executables. When you really get into it, you'll find there are lots of tools provided for you by DOS. You can almost completely automate many of your redundant processes if they occur from the DOS prompt. And you don't have to be a programmer!

Chapter Twelve

HELP Yourself

Microsoft actually included a HELP feature with DOS 5.0. Actually, it's not very elegant, but it's there. Each DOS 5.0 command has some HELP text built into it. In addition, there's a general HELP command, which either displays a list of all DOS commands and a brief description, or just offers help on a specific command. Either way you ask for it, you get help. Oh happy day!

This chapter is about DOS 5.0's HELP command and the help you can get with all DOS commands. Collectively that's referred to as the "HELP facility," though no plumbing is involved.

Using DOS 5.0's HELP Facility

There are two ways to get help at the DOS prompt. One way to get help is to use this syntax:

<COMMAND OR FILE NAME> /?

For example, if you need help for the CLS command, you type CLS /?. The slash-question mark is the universal help switch, available with almost all DOS commands. (A few of the highly technical commands lack the /? option.)

Another way to get help is to use this syntax:

HELP <COMMAND OR FILE NAME>

Just what way you get your help is of course up to you. Here's the help you get when you ask about the COPY command:

C:\DOS>HELP COPY
COPIES ONE OR MORE FILES TO ANOTHER LOCATION.

COPY [/A | /B] SOURCE [/A | /B] [+ SOURCE [/A i /B] [+ . . .]]
[DESTINATION [/A | /B]] [/V]

SOURCE	SPECIFIES THE FILE OR FILES TO BE COPIED.
/A	INDICATES AN ASCII TEXT FILE.
/B	INDICATES A BINARY FILE.
DESTINATION	SPECIFIES THE DIRECTORY AND/OR FILE NAME FOR THE NEW FILE(S).
/V	VERIFIES THAT NEW FILES ARE WRITTEN CORRECTLY.

TO APPEND FILES, SPECIFY A SINGLE FILE FOR DESTINATION, BUT MULTIPLE FILES FOR SOURCE (USING WILDCARDS OR FILE1+FILE2+FILE3 FORMAT).

This is what you can expect for help when you ask for it on the subject of FORMAT.COM. Use this next command to get help on the FORMAT utility:

C:\DOS HELP FORMAT

This is what you get:

FORMATS A DISK FOR USE WITH DOS.

FORMAT DRIVE:	[/V[:LABEL]] [/Q] [/U] [/F:SIZE] [/B |[S]
FORMAT DRIVE:	[/V[:LABEL]] [/Q] [/U] [/T:TRACKS N:SECTORS] [/B | /S]
FORMAT DRIVE:	[/V[:LABEL]] [/Q] [/U] [/1] [/4] [/B | /S]
FORMAT DRIVE:	[/Q] [/U] [/1] [/4] [/8] [/B | /S]
/V[:LABEL]	SPECIFIES THE VOLUME LABEL.
/Q	PERFORMS A QUICK FORMAT.
/U	PERFORMS AN UNCONDITIONAL FORMAT.
/F:SIZE	SPECIFIES THE SIZE OF THE FLOPPY DISK TO FORMAT (SUCH AS 160, 180, 320, 360, 720, 1.2, 1.44, .88).
/B	ALLOCATES SPACE ON THE FORMATTED DISK FOR SYSTEM FILES.
/S	COPIES SYSTEM FILES TO THE FORMATTED DISK.

/T:TRACKS	SPECIFIES THE NUMBER OF TRACKS PER DISK SIDE.
/N:SECTORS	SPECIFIES THE NUMBER OF SECTORS PER TRACK.
/1	FORMATS A SINGLE SIDE OF A FLOPPY DISK.
/4	FORMATS A 5.25-INCH 360K FLOPPY DISK IN A HIGH-DENSITY DRIVE.
/8	FORMATS EIGHT SECTORS PER TRACK.

Using DOSSHELL's HELP

DOSSHELL is a utility included with DOS 5.0 that gives you menu-driven control of the way you work with files and directories on your drives. With DOSSHELL, you don't have to remember most of the commonly used DOS commands. You are provided with menus that let you select from lists of what the commands actually do. If you have trouble remembering DOS commands, or you just plain frustrate yourself to tears with DOS error messages, DOSSHELL may be for you.

There are a lot of products out there that are like DOSSHELL, but they cost money. When you consider the cost of DOS 5.0 and what you get for it, DOSSHELL alone is worth the price. If you want to avoid the DOS prompt without spending additional moollah, DOSSHELL can be the way to go.

The best way to check out DOSSHELL is to run it and run around inside it. All you have to do is type DOSSHELL at the DOS prompt and you'll see DOSSHELL. It looks a lot like the *Windows* File Manager. You can manipulate what drives you look at, how files are displayed, the colors you see, etc.

It's really a great product—especially if you're coming from the DOS-prompt-only environment. DOSSHELL is *wonderful* if you just want to get the job done in the quickest and easiest fashion. You can even run it in a window if you graduate to Microsoft *Windows* and want to stick with DOSSHELL. It can take a little longer to open DOSSHELL in a window unless you maximize the window first. Once you open the program, it will run just fine in a window, but consider invoking it in full-screen mode if your intent is to use it often from *Windows*. Also, it's best to create a PIF file for DOSSHELL to make it work really well.

If you "have a need for speed," as the line from a popular movie goes, configure DOSSHELL for text mode instead of graphics mode. DOSSHELL runs much faster in normal text mode, as do all other programs. In fact, don't be surprised if DOSSHELL actually runs faster from within *Windows* than it does at the DOS prompt.

Let's face it: DOSSHELL's HELP facility is far and above what most would have expected to find. And it sure beats the HELP facility from the DOS prompt. Not only is DOSSHELL's HELP facility multi-indexed, but it's also multi-tiered. Take a look at the general help topics available from the HELP menu item in DOSSHELL:

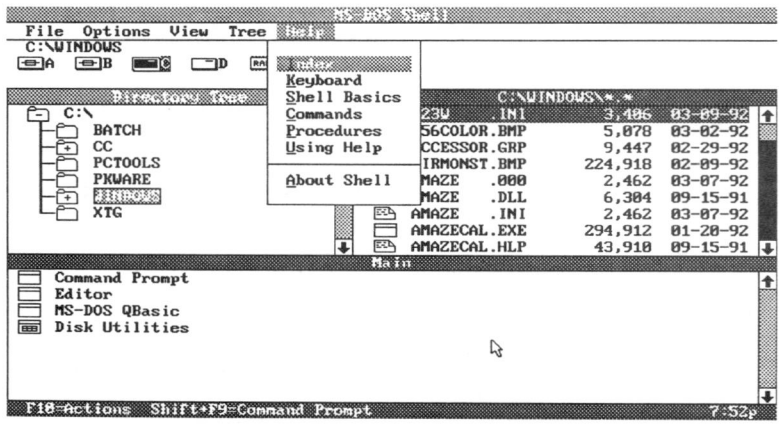

Figure 12.1: The DOSSHELL HELP menu.

DOSSHELL actually allows you to go through a list of topics before it gets into the nitty-gritty. The screen shot on the next page shows a list of topics that you can choose from the subject of working with the keyboard.

If you are unclear on the subject of starting programs right from DOSSHELL without using the DOS prompt, you just double-click on the program's name with the mouse, or scroll though the list of

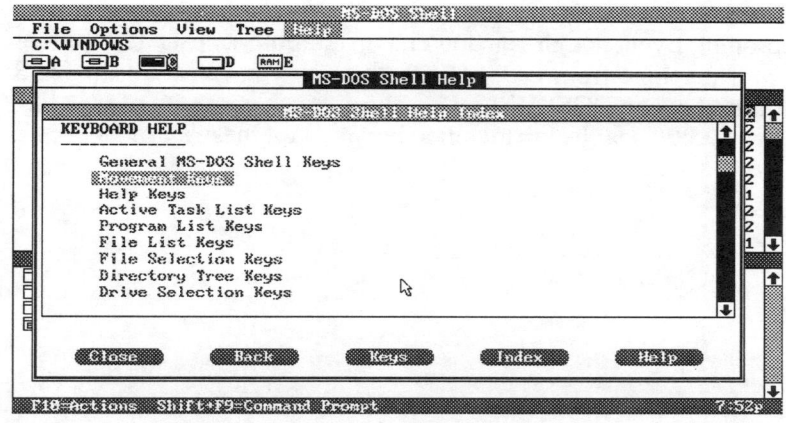

Figure 12.2: One of the first topic levels: Keyboards.

available files in the directory with the arrow keys. The next figure shows you the kind of step-by-step procedure help you'll get when using DOSSHELL HELP:

The only thing about DOSSHELL that you may find disconcerting is that its HELP facility does not give separate help text on each of the commands that can be run from the DOS prompt. Its HELP facility is geared toward using DOSSHELL, not the DOS

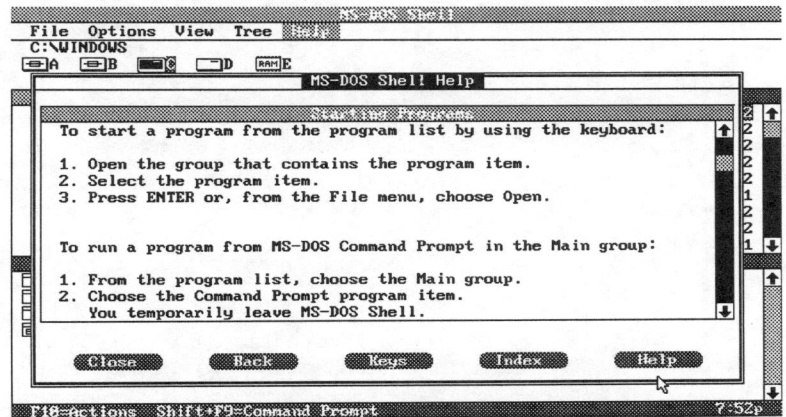

Figure 12.3: Help with starting programs from DOSSHELL.

prompt. Even though you don't have the ability to pseudo-program your machine from DOSSHELL the way you can from the DOS prompt, using DOSSHELL can take as much stress out of your day as a $2,000 health club membership. And for the price of DOS 5.0!

Chapter Thirteen
Windows *Secrets*

Like all software documentation, *Windows* 3.1's does not "win" awards for clarity and simplicity. Historically compared, DOS 5.0 and *Windows* 3.1 documentation is among the best to come out of the industry. That's the good news.

In this chapter, we'll talk about what can be done to make you a happier *Windows* user without adding any additional cost. There really are a wealth of utilities and features that come with DOS 5.0 when used in tandem with *Windows* 3.1. *Windows* 3.1, by nature of design, will not be for everybody, however.

Graphical Computing

Graphical computing is clearly the coming "rage." With the advent of *Windows* and the growing popularity of '386 computing, more and more people are turning to graphical computing to help make computing just plain *less work*.

It's actually more fun by far than character-based computing. You just plain can't beat seeing exactly what you're getting in hard copy before you print it.

If the ease of use is not enough to sell you, think about the options. You can use any of hundreds of typestyles in your documents as long as you use a modern application designed to run with *Windows*.

When the big kids on the market-share block, like WordPerfect Corporation and Lotus Development, release versions of their software that are essentially ported renditions of their DOS or character-based products, you know what graphical interface users are saying has to be true: Graphical computing is clearly the coming "rage."

Windows Modes of Operation

With version 3.0, *Windows* gave you the option of running in three distinctly different modes. The first, real mode, is intended to run on an XT. The second, standard mode, was designed for 80286 computers. And everything above that on the microprocessor evolutionary scale runs *Windows* in its ultra deluxe '386 enhanced mode.

Real Mode

Real mode, intended to run on an XT, will only address 1 megabyte of memory. Real mode is the normal state of the 8088 CPU. There is no such thing as multitasking in real mode.

Some early kludges (workarounds) were accomplished in the latter days of the XT to provide over 1 megabyte of memory, but they proved to be too unreliable. Those seeking dependable memory management above the 1,024K mark would have to look elsewhere.

Today, the only version of *Windows* that is current, and operates on an XT is *Windows* 3.0. *Windows* 3.1 will not run in *real mode*.

Standard Mode

Standard mode (as far as *Windows* is concerned) allows you to multitask *Windows* applications. Standard mode is available with both *Windows* 3.0 and *Windows* 3.1. You must have 1 megabyte of memory to run in standard mode. You cannot, however, run DOS applications in a window at the same time you are running *Windows* applications.

The 80286 processor was introduced in 1984 to replace the 8088, or XT. The 80286 will run in real mode and standard mode. Remember, *Windows* 3.1 does not support real mode, or operation on an XT. Unfortunately, '286s can't switch between real and standard mode when you try to run both types of applications in *Windows*. True multitasking has had to wait for the 80386.

The AT 80286 had three distinct advantages over the XT. The first was the fact that it could operate in *protected mode*. This meant that the 80286 could:

- Access up to 16 megabytes of memory
- Allow operation of protected mode software
- Support virtual drives of over 1 gigabyte in size.

The second benefit was that the 80286 AT offered a 16-bit bus. The 16-bit data path on the system bus meant that data could be transferred to and from the plug-in cards at twice the rate of the XT.

The third benefit of the 80286 AT over the XT was sheer speed. The processor was capable of operating at about twice the effective overall speed of the XTs. Later versions of the AT actually achieved performance levels of more than 20 times the original XT's benchmarks. By this time though, the 80386 had made its entry, changing computing forever.

'386 Enhanced Mode

'386 enhanced mode allows you to run DOS applications on a '386 in a window at the same time as you're running *Windows* applications. You can run as many DOS and *Windows* applications as you have system memory and resources to do so. The 80386 can switch between real mode and protected mode in order to run older software in a window. The '286 cannot do this. You must have 2 megabytes of memory in an 80386 to use *Windows* properly in '386 enhanced mode.

OK, let's get serious here. To really make *Windows* shine, it needs 4 MB—one gob—of memory. If you can afford it, equip your *Windows* PC with 8 MB of memory. While you're at it, consider a '486 computer as your *Windows* "platform." A '386 or '386SX is fine, but *Windows* can use all the power you can afford. (If you have a '386 or '386SX, consider buying a math coprocessor as a practical way to improve *Windows* speed.)

Which Mode Is for Me?

The mode in which you should run *Windows* depends on a few variables.

The first variable is which machine you own:

- If you own an XT, you must run *Windows* 3.0 in real mode.
- If you own an 80286, you can run *Windows* 3.0 or 3.1 in standard mode only.
- If you own an 80386, you can run *Windows* 3.0 in real, standard and '386 enhanced mode, or *Windows* 3.1 in standard or '386 enhanced mode.

Another variable is the amount of memory you have:

- An XT must run in real mode, regardless of the memory it has at its disposal.
- An 80286 must run in standard mode regardless of the memory it has available.
- An 80386 can run in standard mode if it has at least 1 megabyte of memory, but 2 megabytes is recommended.
- An 80386 can run in '386 enhanced mode if it can access at least 1 megabyte of memory, but at least 2 are recommended. In fact, if you intend to run DOS and *Windows* applications concurrently in *Windows*, you will want 4 megabytes of memory. Any less will afford slower, unacceptable performance results.

Windows actually helps you make the choice. If you have an 80286 with at least 1 megabyte of memory, *Windows* starts in standard mode. If you have an 80386 with 1 megabyte of memory, *Windows* senses this and starts in standard mode. If *Windows* finds a '386 with at least 2 megabytes of memory, it starts in '386 enhanced mode.

You can force *Windows* to start in either mode if you have the hardware to support the two modes by using these two command-line switches after the WIN command to start *Windows*:

- Use WIN /S to start *Windows* in standard mode.
- Type WIN /3 to make *Windows* start in '386 enhanced mode.

Controlling the Windows

This section describes how to work with the windows within *Windows*. Every *Windows* program runs in its own particular window. Most programs will open additional windows within their own application window. It's best to think of these two types of windows as *program* and *document* windows.

Windows allows you to place more objects on your screen than any environment before it. The power is destructive if you let it be. You can clutter up your screen pretty easily until you get a hold of yourself.

Windows 3.1 comes with several bit maps that you can use as a desktop or background behind everything you see on your screen. Though interesting and colorful, some of them are extremely *busy*. You can quickly lose the readability of your icon titles when programs are minimized on a bit map that looks like the floor of a forest in Fall. If you find your screen is too busy using your current wallpaper, click on the Desktop icon from the Control Panel to select another wallpaper, or none, if that makes you happier. Remember, the bit maps that come with *Windows* are really very small pictures. They are usually less than an inch or two across. You need to tile them in order to cover the whole screen.

Selecting Wallpaper

Open the Control Panel and press Alt-D, or double-click on the Desktop icon. Press Alt-F, or click in the Wallpaper File text box. Press Alt-DownArrow to see a drop-down list box of available bit map files. Use the arrow keys to scroll through the list until the file you want is highlighted. If you don't want to make a change to the Tile or Center setting, press the Enter key now.

If you want to change the setting so that the bit map floats in the center of your screen, click on the "Center" radio button or press Alt-C. If you would like *Windows* to paste the bit map across the screen starting at the top-left portion of your display (until the screen is filled with your bit map), make sure you've clicked on the "Tile" radio button or pressed Alt-C. If you've made any changes to the Tile and Center settings you'll need to click on the OK button or just press the Enter key to save your selections.

Making Your Own Wallpaper

You can make *your own* wallpaper rather easily, as well. All you need is a graphics file in the *Windows* bit-map (BMP) format to display as wallpaper. *Windows Paintbrush* will let you paint and save to a BMP format.

You can even paste into a BMP file from the *Windows* Clipboard while running *Paintbrush*. This nifty little angle is great for capturing any screen with the PrintScrn key, and then pasting the captured screen into a new *Paintbrush* file. Crop it down or gussy it up, then save it in the BMP format! Next, copy it into the *Windows* directory.

Open Control Panel. You can press Alt-D to open the Desktop dialog box, or you can double-click on the Desktop icon and in the Wallpaper section; select the bit-map file you just made. Select either Tile or Center and save your changes by clicking on the OK button. You should now see your home-made bit map on your screen in the way you asked *Windows* to display it.

Some people actually design their own business cards and display them in this fashion. Network administrators use this feature to display messages and warnings regarding network etiquette. Many people also use this feature to display scanned versions of their favorite *Larson* cartoons! Of course, your company's logo can be displayed in the same way (you company *person*, you), or a reminder note can save your hide: displaying the *date of your upcoming anniversary.*

The Hard Way

You can avoid using the Control Panel by editing your WIN.INI file manually. You can open NotePad and the WIN.INI file, or you can create and double-click on the SYSEDIT.EXE icon. SYSEDIT is like the NotePad program, but it opens four document windows: AUTOEXEC.BAT, CONFIG.SYS, WIN.INI and SYSTEM.INI. However you do it, make WIN.INI the active or foreground window, and find the [Desktop] section. It   ook like this:

    [Desktop]
    Pattern=(None)
    Wallpaper=zigzag.bm

```
GridGranularity=0
IconSpacing=60
TileWallPaper=1
```

Look for the Wallpaper= setting. We'll show you the heading and section with the Wallpaper= setting in bold text:

```
[Desktop]
Pattern=(None)
```
Wallpaper=zigzag.bmp
```
GridGranularity=0
IconSpacing=60
TileWallPaper=1
```

Simply substitute the name of your preferred bit-map file for the current one. Leave no spaces in the setting statement. That's all there is to it. Save the file, and close—then reopen—*Windows*.

Unlike using the Control Panel's Desktop dialog box to make this change, you don't get instant gratification from using this shortcut. The Desktop dialog box makes the change immediate. You need to rerun *Windows* whenever you make a manual change to the WIN.INI file.

At least when you show your friends how to do this you can say you didn't read the directions!

Working With Windows

Fortunately, you can handle program and document windows in the same way. The tasks you usually perform on windows include moving them around the screen, making them larger and smaller, and switching between windows. When you're finished with a window, you normally close it. You can even take the easy way out and press the Alt-F4 key to panic-close the application running in the foreground!

There are many *Windows* screen objects that you will get to know as you work with *Windows*. Objects are parts of the *Windows* screen that serve a distinct purpose, but are only called upon when appropriate.

Opening Windows

When a program opens more than one document window, only one of them is *active* at any one time. When you do something, it affects only the active window; the inactive windows just sit there until you activate one of them. You can tell which window is active by looking at the color of the title bars. For most color combinations, the active window title bar is colored or shaded differently than the title bar on an inactive window.

The method you use to make a window active depends on the program you're using. As far as *Windows* is concerned, the active window is always in the *foreground*. You can toggle document windows into the foreground with the Alt-F6 keystroke combo.

Moving Windows Around

You can usually move a document or file window anywhere within the program's application window. With some applications, you can often move some document windows off the edge of the application window so that only a small part of the document window is visible. Don't try this with *NotePad* or *Paintbrush*. You can shift an application window to anywhere else on the desktop by dragging the Title Bar with your mouse.

Recessing Your Windows

Changing the size of a window is very much like moving a window. When you re-size a particular window, you can move one of the edges in or out while the other edges remain stationary. This makes the window change size.

You can change the placement of two window sides at one time. When you place your pointer over the corner of a window, you see a double-headed arrow. Drag the double-headed arrow to where you want it, and then release the mouse button. Changing the size of a window at a window's corner is a lot faster than re-sizing two edges separately.

Scrolling Inside Windows

When the contents of a window are larger than the window itself, you will see *scroll bars* appear at the right and/or bottom of the window. Sorry keyboard lovers, scroll bars require a mouse.

To move up the information in the window using the mouse, point at the down-arrow symbol or button at the top of the scroll bar and press on the mouse button. To move the contents down, use the up-arrow button. The horizontal scroll bar works the same way, and is especially useful for viewing large spreadsheets.

As you scroll, you can tell where you are in the document by looking at the position markers, or the *scroll box* (the square that moves along the scroll bar). When the scroll box is at the top of the scroll bar, you see the beginning of the file; when it is near the middle, you see the middle of the file; when it is near the bottom, you see the end of the contents.

If you want to scroll faster, click in the area between the up and down arrows, and the scroll box makes the contents move one full window at a time. If the window contains a great deal of data, this is an even faster way to see it all: Some programs move the position in the file relative to the point where you click on the scroll bar, not just one window at a time.

With a lot of *Windows* programs, the item you selected in the window remains the same until you finish moving the box *and* let go of the mouse button. Some programs even let you drag the scroll box along the scroll bar, moving the contents of the files up or down as you do so. You will see this feature more and more in coming *Windows* products. Users like the feature, and software developers are getting the message. How novel.

Vertical and horizontal scroll bars work the same way. If you're a big word processor user, you probably scroll vertically through your documents. If you use a drawing program, you probably scroll both horizontally and vertically in your drawings.

Maximizing Windows

Moving and re-sizing windows can take a lot of time if what you really want to do is maximize the active window by making a window as large as possible. For example, when you're working in a word processing program, you probably want the program's window to be as large as the screen and the document window you're working in to be as large as you can make it.

Maximizing a window is just like dragging the upper-left corner of the window to the far top-left corner of the screen and dragging the bottom-right corner as far down and to the right as you can swing it—except that the application window border often disappears entirely.

When you maximize a particular window, *Windows* keeps track of the shape of the window before maximization. You can *restore* the window to that size and shape in one step by single-clicking the double triangle button in the upper-right portion of a program or document window.

Minimizing Document Windows

At one time or another, most people want to place windows out of the way without actually closing them. In this case, you may want to make the window as small as is practical while keeping it visible so that you can get at it when you want it. This is called *minimizing* the window.

Some *Windows* applications minimize document or file windows by changing them into icons and placing them along the outside edge of the application window. Some *Windows* programs (like Microsoft's flagship, *Word for Windows*) don't let you minimize document or file windows; they only let you toggle between them, tile them or close them entirely. Although the motions you make to minimize program windows are the same as minimizing document windows, what you end up with is very different.

The Dialog Boxes

Many *Windows* programs have menu commands that open dialog boxes from which you can select options for the commands. In *Windows*, dialog boxes are the standard way to talk back to the program.

There are many ways to talk back to a *Windows* program using dialog boxes. Some dialog boxes use a combination of list boxes, command buttons, and check boxes. You can make the selections with the mouse or the keyboard. Many people learn that making choices with the mouse can be much faster than the keyboard, unless the dialog box has very few options.

The Amazing Clipboard

The *Windows* Clipboard stores just one piece of information at a time. This data or information can be either text or graphics in one form or another. The Clipboard is a storage buffer that's filled when you tell *Windows* to copy something to the Clipboard. Since there are a lot of applications that will rely on moving data between applications, Microsoft developed a standard from which developers can create totally compliant applications with a minimum of problems. Microsoft calls the standard the "DDE" or Dynamic Data Exchange. The DDE standard assures that data can be passed between applications properly. The ability to pass data between totally foreign applications is new for the PC. This feature really helps to cut redundant entry of data in applications. The Clipboard will store as much data as your system's memory will allow.

Clipboard Viewer, on the other hand, is a small program that displays what you've got in the Clipboard buffer. Many DOS programs can transact data to and from the Clipboard if you're using *Windows* 3.1. The Clipboard Viewer is run like any other program—by clicking on its icon. Clipboard Viewer can be maximized, minimized or closed without losing or damaging the data in the Clipboard's buffer.

The Clipboard has two common uses:

- To cut and paste information from one part of a file to another.
- To cut and paste information from one program to another.

As soon as you put an item in the Clipboard, it's going to stay there until you place another item in the Clipboard or until you quit *Windows*. If you want, you can dump the contents of the Clipboard to free up memory by selecting the Edit Delete command from the Clipboard Viewer's menu.

Remember that the Clipboard is run by *Windows*, not individual programs. This makes it a lot more powerful. Virtually all programs work well using the contents of the Clipboard. That's because the Clipboard senses the format of the data (as in file format) and saves the data to the buffer in the same format, if it recognizes it. This is called the *owner* format, or the format used by the originating application. The data is kept there in the owner's format until it is needed or you delete it, reboot, or power-down the machine.

One biggy to remember about the Clipboard is that it holds only one piece of data at a time. You can't place two things on the Clipboard and expect to find them both there when you use Clipboard Viewer to see them.

Using the Clipboard's Contents

Just about every *Windows* program has an Edit menu. Most Edit menus contain three commands: Edit Cut, Edit Copy, and Edit Paste. These commands work in virtually the same way for every *Windows* program.

The Edit Cut and Edit Copy commands in your application's Edit menu place information in the Clipboard. The big difference between these commands is that Edit Cut removes the information from the document when it puts it in the Clipboard, and the Edit Copy command leaves the *selected* image in the document. Generally, you use the Edit Cut command to move information and the Edit Copy command to duplicate it.

To put the contents of the Clipboard into your document, use the Edit Paste command. This command copies the Clipboard contents into the document at the currently selected point. Note that the Edit Paste command does not clear the contents of the Clipboard: It's still there for you to use again.

What the Clipboard Can Hold

Two types of information can be stored in the Clipboard: text and graphics. When you use the Edit Cut or Edit Copy commands, *Windows* looks at the information you've selected in the program you're running and stores whatever it can.

If you're using a basic text editor like Notepad, you copy plain text to the Clipboard. If you are using a more advanced program, such as *Write*, you copy formatted text. Similarly, if you use a simple paint program, such as *Paintbrush*, you copy only a *bit map* of the picture (a copy of the pixels) you see on the screen.

While running a program, the Clipboard holds text with formatting information or graphics with objects. In fact, if you are using a program like *Write* that enables you to have both text and graphics in a single document, you can have both text and graphics in the Clipboard at one time. The Clipboard is not famous for pasting perfectly formatted text when it is stored with graphics, though, so experiment with your system to determine the best attainable results.

As soon as you quit from a program, the information in the Clipboard is reduced to either just text or just a bit map (graphics image). All formatting and special objects are lost. In fact, even if the program is still running and you've switched to another program, that extra information still might be lost. In this case, you can transfer only pure text or a single bit map to another program. Again, this depends on what features the software manufacturer built into the program.

You can copy information from non-*Windows* or text-based programs to the Clipboard, although in a much more limited fashion than when copying between graphical, or *Windows* programs. The Clipboard Viewer program in the Main group window of Program Manager enables you to view the contents of the Clipboard. When there is nothing in the Clipboard, such as when you first start *Windows*, the Display menu is dimmed.

Clipboard Files

Clipboard files are useful for saving the contents of the Clipboard if you are about to replace the Clipboard contents with other information. These files are of limited value if you must use them often, because you have to remember what is in each file by name—you can't "preview" the contents. Also, because the files save only text or bit maps, they aren't useful for storing complex information.

The File Exit command closes Clipboard Viewer. The data in the Clipboard will stay intact if you haven't rebooted your computer or cleared the Clipboard.

Clearing the Clipboard

The Edit Delete command clears the contents of the Clipboard. This command is rarely useful because it doesn't hurt to leave the contents in the Clipboard until the next time you give an Edit Cut or Edit Copy command. You might want to use the Edit Delete command if you are low on memory and you have a large picture or lots of text in the Clipboard.

Looking Into It

Based on the kind of information you have in the Clipboard, there are several ways to display it. The Display menu changes, based on the kind of information in the Clipboard.

When a menu item is not available to you, it's *grayed out*. When there's data in the Clipboard, the Display Auto command is always available.

If you want to look at *text*, you have two options: Display Text and Display OEM (Original Equipment Manufacturer) Text. The difference between these two is the font that's used to display the text in the Clipboard window. The Display Text command shows the text in the display font, which would normally be a proportional font.

If you're running a program that handles formatted text or complex graphics, there may be more display options available to you. If the application is 100 percent DDE compliant, you'll see the Display Owner Display command. This command makes the viewable content in the Clipboard appear the same as the creating application displays it.

Based on the program, you might have other options in the Display menu. *Word for Windows* uses a format for text called RTF (Rich Text Format).

RTF is a file formatted with all the embedded format symbols (line feeds, spaces, tabs, and so on) intact and in place. When you copy text to the Clipboard from *Word for Windows*, the data is saved to the Clipboard in RTF format and text format, so that you view both from the Display menu.

Uses for the Clipboard

Whenever you want to transfer data from one application to another, you could use the Clipboard. You might not be able to transfer all the information you want, but in most cases you can transfer text or bit maps between any two *Windows* applications.

Working With DOS Programs

If you use File Manager more than Program Manager, you might want to start your non-*Windows* programs directly from File Manager. You can start any non-*Windows* program, including batch files, from File Manager. You can start programs with the extensions EXE, COM, BAT, and PIF.

Using the DOS Prompt Icon

When you use the DOS prompt icon in the main window of Program Manager, you can run programs from the DOS command line. The DOS prompt icon puts up a window with a standard DOS prompt. You then can run programs as you normally would in DOS.

When you're finished with the DOS session, you must give the EXIT command at the DOS prompt. Otherwise, the DOS session will continue indefinitely. Unless you change the settings in your DOS PIF file, this is the only way to finish a DOS-prompt session.

When running a DOS-prompt session, be sure not to delete or alter any files that are being used to run *Windows*. Doing so can cause your PC to crash. That means lost data or even fragmented files. Also, be sure not to run commands that change the parts of the disk that *Windows* uses, like a disk-compaction utility. *Windows lets you know this is a no-no* in many cases.

In general, you shouldn't delete any files in the *Windows* directory while running *Windows*, because this action can cause unpredictable results. This fact is particularly true when you run non-*Windows* programs, because *Windows* will expect all files to be available when you return to DOS and will crash if they are not there.

Not Enough Environment Space?

You may get this error message when you start a DOS session or run a batch file in an DOS session:

OUT OF ENVIRONMENT SPACE

Environment space is memory allocated to store environment variables. Unless you specify exactly how much environment space you need, DOS gives you a very small amount. When you start a new DOS session, that session gets a copy of all the environment variables, but only a minor amount of space to which it can add variables.

You can increase the amount of environment space by using program parameters. The best way to do this is in the PIF for the icon you use to start the DOS session. Use the /E parameter in the Program Parameters section of the PIF to reserve space.

The syntax you use for the /E parameter depends on the version of DOS you are using. In DOS version 3.2 or higher, you specify the number of bytes in the /E parameter. In DOS version 3.1, you specify the number of units of 16 bytes, not the number of bytes themselves.

Changing Your DOS Prompt

When you run the DOS prompt from *Windows*, you can forget that you're running from within *Windows*. This can be a real pain.

- You might restart your computer with *Windows* applications still open and lose whatever data is being held by SMARTDrive, instead of returning to *Windows* and quitting from *Windows* by closing all applications first.

To remind yourself that you're running *Windows*, you should change the look of your DOS prompt. For example, you might want to keep the same prompt but add EXIT to the beginning of the prompt to remind you to use the EXIT command to return to your graphical environment.

To automatically add a reminder to your prompt, follow these steps:

1. Create a batch file that contains these three lines:

```
ECHO OFF
PROMPT USE "EXIT"!: %PROMPT%
%COMSPEC%
```

You can use any text editor, like Notepad, to create a batch file. You can change the text that appears at the beginning of the prompt by making the %PROMPT% command in the second line append your current prompt.

2. Save this batch file to disk. Call the file EXIT.BAT.
3. Now run the PIF Editor.
4. The two optional parameters are important options to COMMAND.COM. /E:500 indicates that you want an environment space of 500 bytes. If you have the /E parameter in your CONFIG.SYS file, the amount of memory you allocate here should be greater (because you're adding text to the PROMPT string). The /C parameter tells DOS to run the batch file to change the prompt to the one you just made.
5. Save the PIF to disk. Name the file something that will help you remember why it's around, like EXIT.PIF.
6. Now create an icon for this PIF. If you want, you can choose one from the MOREICON.DLL file that comes with *Windows* 3.1. Whenever you run this special DOS icon, you'll get the prompt you just created. You can add whatever you want to the batch file. For example, if there is a TSR you want to run only when starting DOS programs from *Windows*, you can also add it to the other lines in the batch file.

Operating Modes and DOS Programs

The way you view non-*Windows* programs and the way *Windows* handles these programs depends on the operating mode you use. You need to know which operating mode you're running—and the best way to find out is to check out the Help About dialog box from Program Manager.

Using Standard Mode

In standard mode, all non-*Windows* programs run full-screen; that is, you cannot run a character-based program in a window.

Using '386 Enhanced Mode

In '386 enhanced mode, you can run several text-based programs in their own windows. When you run text-based programs, *Windows* can continue to run other *Windows* programs in the background. If you run *Windows* in '386 enhanced mode, you can specify that text-based programs run in their own windows rather than full-screen. Note that you cannot run graphics-based non-*Windows* programs in their own window: They must run full-screen. Some combination-based (text and graphics) programs can run in a window with no problem. You need to experiment to find out if yours will run this way.

When you run a combination-based program in a window, you must not switch to graphics mode. Even if you don't switch to graphics mode, *Windows* might give you an error message when you quit from the program, as described in the next section.

To tell *Windows* 3.1 that you want a DOS program to start in its own window in '386 enhanced mode, use the PIF Editor. Change the Display Usage choice from Full Screen to Windowed and save the changes to the PIF.

1. Choose Settings from the control menu in that program's window.

2. Change Display Options setting from Window to the Full Screen setting.

3. Click the OK button to save the settings.

Some Pitfalls

Changing to Windowed (vs. full-screen) mode works for many text-based programs, but it doesn't work for some graphics-based programs. Even if you can start the combination-based program appropriately, you might still have problems when you leave the program.

If *Windows* detects a graphics-based element in a program you're starting in a window (or a program you are switching to Windowed mode by pressing Alt-Enter) you may see a dialog box with the following message:

- You cannot run this application in a window or in the background.

- You can display it in a window, but it will be suspended until you run it full screen. Check the PIF settings to ensure they are correct.

If you see this message, click the OK button and switch back to full-screen mode. If *Windows* shows the same alert when the program is exiting, click the OK button. After you take the steps just mentioned, you might see an inactive window. You must close this inactive window from its control menu. Until you do, each time you press a key, *Windows* will beep at you.

DOS TSRs

It's not unusual for people switching to *Windows* to be reliant on TSR programs they were using under DOS. These TSRs fall into two overall categories:

- Background device drivers or handlers such as network programs and mouse drivers.

- Pop-up utilities available at all times.

Background device drivers are almost always loaded in your AUTOEXEC.BAT and CONFIG.SYS files when you start your computer. You don't need to "start" them again when you run *Windows* because they're already running. Most of these devices are useful to you only when you're not running *Windows*, so you might want to judge whether you really need them. Of course, there is a cost involved when you're considering going graphical. You can ease this burden if you run your text-based TSRs from *Windows*, but *Windows* may trap the keystrokes that you used to use for hot keys to invoke the TSR.

If you have devices that must be run even though you're running *Windows*, you should not put the device driver in your CONFIG.SYS file because this wastes RAM for all your DOS programs. Instead, create a file called WINPUT.BAT in your *Windows* directory that contains a line that loads the device driver.

You can create a batch file with the Notepad program or any other ASCII text editor. The documentation included with the driver should have instructions for the syntax to use. The WINPUT.BAT file is loaded only when you start *Windows* in '386 enhanced mode, so the device doesn't waste RAM when you are not running *Windows*.

Using Handy Utilities

Windows treats pop-up utilities like other DOS programs. Thus, you should start them from within *Windows* the same way you start other non-*Windows* programs. Be sure to create a PIF for the utility. As soon as you have loaded a pop-up utility in memory, it stays in memory until you quit *Windows*.

After you've started a pop-up utility, you activate it the same way you would activate it under DOS by pressing its special key combination. The only exceptions to this rule are utilities that use keystrokes used by *Windows*, such as Alt-Tab and Ctrl-Esc. If you have trouble activating a pop-up utility because it conflicts with *Windows* keystrokes, follow these steps:

1. Run the PIF Editor.
2. Open the PIF file for the utility.
3. In the Reserve Shortcut Keys section, choose the key that you need to activate the utility. If you run in '386 enhanced mode, you must click the Advanced button to see this section. Choosing a key tells *Windows* not to use that key for itself when that program is running.
4. Save the changes to the PIF.
5. Quit from *Windows*.
6. Restart *Windows* to effect the changes.

Application Switching

Non-*Windows* programs act the same as *Windows* programs after you have started them. You use the same actions to switch between programs. To switch to or from a non-*Windows* program, press Alt-Esc or use the Task Manager.

Data Transfer and Non-*Windows* Programs

Windows is weakest in passing information to and from non-*Windows* programs. As with *Windows* programs, you use the Clipboard to transfer information. The type of information you can put into the Clipboard or retrieve from the Clipboard is very limited, though.

The information you can copy to the Clipboard depends on the mode you run in and what type of non-*Windows* program you're running. Note that if you run in standard mode and your program is graphics-based, you cannot copy anything from that program to the Clipboard.

Copying Text and Pictures

If you run in '386 enhanced mode, and you are running in a window, you can copy a bit-mapped picture of the entire window to the Clipboard by pressing Alt-PrintScrn. You can't copy the text on the screen as text in the Clipboard if you run in standard mode.

If you run in '386 Enhanced mode, and you are running in a window, you can copy text from your program to the Clipboard. This is a great way to copy text information to *Windows* programs. To do this, you must use commands from the Edit cascading menu in the window's control menu.

Copying Pictures of the Screen

When you run a text-based non-*Windows* program and you are running full-screen, you can copy a bit-mapped picture of the entire screen to the Clipboard by pressing the PrintScrn key on your keyboard. If the PrintScrn key does not copy the screen to the Clipboard, try Shift-PrintScrn or Alt-PrintScrn.

If you run in '386 enhanced mode and your non-*Windows* program is graphics-based, you can copy a picture of the screen to the Clipboard by pressing PrintScrn. Pressing the PrintScrn key when you are running *Windows* causes the image on your screen to be saved to the Clipboard; it does not go to your printer. You can look at it by running Clipboard Viewer, and you can print it if you paste the contents of the Clipboard (your screen image) into any application (like *Windows Write*) that will accept its contents into a document. This is a pain. Let's hope Microsoft fixes this and allows printing directly from the Clipboard in future versions of *Windows*.

You can also copy highlighted portions of a text-based application's screen to the Clipboard by selecting the Edit Mark menu item from the DOS window's control menu. *Windows* will let you copy a highlighted selection to the Clipboard, or let you paste the contents of the Clipboard into a text-based document if the receiving application will accept it.

In either case, you can paste the results of your copying into any *Windows* program that can handle graphics. You can paste copied *text* into a DOS application. You *cannot* paste a graphic back into a non-*Windows* program.

Some Insights Into Memory Usage

Many situations might keep *Windows* from starting a non-*Windows* program due to lack of memory. We should say that this problem is different from not having enough memory to run a *Windows* program. There are two ways to get a program running in a low-memory situation:

- Free up memory in *Windows*.
- Reduce the amount of memory the program needs.

You can set the amount of memory a program needs in its PIF. You should be careful when reducing this amount, because although most programs will start all right, they may crash later if they have too little memory.

If you run in '386 enhanced mode, you can slightly reduce the memory requirement for a program by simply running the program full-screen instead of in its own window. You can change the setting for this in the program's PIF.

You also can change whether a program runs full-screen as it's running with a keystroke combination. Just press Ctrl-Enter to toggle between full-screen and windows operation.

What Can Go Wrong

Despite all of its improvements over the previous version, *Windows* 3.1 still leaves us with some things to be desired. Absolute no-brainer simplicity is still to be achieved by our friends at Microsoft. Until *Windows* and DOS are in effect *combined*, as they are in OS/2, we'll have to live with the problems of using a graphical environment that has to deal with an underlying text-based disk operating system. This section contains advice both weak and strong, about some pitfalls to reckon with.

Good Thinking

Although all non-*Windows* programs are supposed to work fine under *Windows*, often they do not. Your computer can crash, forcing you to reboot your system or at least quit the program unexpectedly. The following tips, although inconvenient, should reduce the number of problems you have running non-*Windows* programs.

- Minimize *Windows* programs before running a non-*Windows* program. This returns a little more memory to the environment's available memory pool and reduces the chance that a *Windows* program will do something unexpected in the background. Ever share a joint checking account with each user carrying a separate checkbook? Think about it.

- Do not run non-*Windows* programs when backing up your hard disk with a *Windows* backup program.

- Do not run non-*Windows* programs from *Windows* in the background in '386 enhanced mode. Many programs will crash, sometimes locking up your entire system. Whammo!

- Use the latest version available of HIMEM.SYS for your extended memory management. Even though some commercial products are better, most program makers have tested their non-*Windows* programs only with HIMEM.SYS.
- Run only one non-*Windows* program at a time. Making *Windows* juggle more than one program can cause the two programs to conflict—not to mention slowing your system to a snail's pace.
- If you do not need to access files on the network while you run non-*Windows* programs, boot your system without the network software. This gives the programs more memory and reduces the chance of a device contention problem.

Risky Business

Unfortunately, there are many DOS commands you should never run *while* you are running *Windows*. These commands can cause unpredictable results for many reasons. In fact, some can cause you to lose files from your hard disk. The dangerous programs you shouldn't run while running *Windows* include the following commands:

- APPEND
- FASTOPEN
- FORMAT
- JOIN
- SHARE
- SUBST

Switching From Non-Windows Programs

Many things can prevent you from switching from a non-*Windows* program when you press Alt-Tab, Alt-Esc, or Ctrl-Esc. This section should help you determine just what is keeping you from switching.

The most common reason for not being able to switch using one of the key combinations is that the program's PIF has reserved the combination for itself. Quit from the program and edit the PIF to check whether any of the combinations are reserved.

Another common reason is that the program's PIF specifies the wrong video mode for the program. Quit from the program and change the PIF to the correct video setting.

Two other PIF settings can prevent you from switching from the program. As you might imagine, setting the *Prevent Program Switch* option in the PIF would keep you from switching. Surprise! The *Directly Modifies* options act the same as the *Prevent Program Switch* option because you can't switch from a program that modifies hardware until that hardware is freed by quitting the program. In either of these cases, you can't leave the program without quitting.

Another reason you might not be able to switch is that the program uses a video mode that *Windows* doesn't know about. If *Windows* can't save the contents of the screen, it doesn't switch from the program. This situation is sort of rare because *Windows* knows about almost every video mode used in almost every common PC program.

If a non-*Windows* program has the *Prevent Program Switch* or a *Directly Modifies* option set *on* in the PIF that comes with it, do not edit the PIF to turn off these options. The program probably will run but might cause *Windows* to act unpredictably or crash.

A few older DOS programs take all the keyboard input from other programs, even *Windows*. In this case, you can't use the Alt-Tab, Alt-Esc, or Ctrl-Esc keys to switch from the program. You need to quit the program in the usual fashion first. If a DOS program re-maps the keyboard for its own keystroke combinations, some of the *Windows* keystroke combinations may be superseded when you are running that DOS program.

Getting More on Your Screen

If your video card and monitor support high-resolution mode, you can now change the way your system displays information entirely from within *Windows* with version 3.1. The benefit of working in a higher-resolution mode is that you can get more windows and icons on your screen at any one time. You can have more windows open, more icons in each window, and more text visible while editing a document if you go up one or two levels of resolution.

The Setup program can be run in one of two ways: One runs when you double-click on the Setup icon from within *Windows* and the other runs from the DOS prompt. It's the easiest way to change how your monitor displays differing resolution levels from within *Windows* 3.1.

When you selected VGA from the Setup program as you installed *Windows*, a line in your SYSTEM.INI file was modified to reflect the name of the driver that would provide you with 640-by-480 resolution (if you have a VGA monitor).

800-by-600 Mode

If you were one of the many people who recently purchased an 800 by 600 or 1024 (8514/A) monitor, you may be able to get more on your screen than you are now. The two common modes above 640 by 480 are 800 by 600 and 1024 by 768.

To use the 800-by-600 mode, your monitor must be of the multisync variety or a *multiscanning* monitor. The manual provided with your monitor should indicate if the monitor supports 800-by-600 resolution.

If the video card supports the higher resolutions as well, the upgrade to 800 by 600 is simpler than some people realize. You may find you like 640 by 480 better, because colors may be more vivid, text may be more readable, and your screen refreshes somewhat faster; you can always go back to 640 by 480 if you choose. The *Windows* 3.1 800-by-600 screen driver is one of the fastest drivers available from anyone. You may not recognize any decrease in speed when you use this driver, but some people do—it depends on the speed of your video card.

It's wise to make a backup copy of your SYSTEM.INI file before you change it, just in case you make a mistake when you're editing the file. Be careful that you don't change *anything else* in the SYSTEM.INI file. You can make a one-letter mistake in the spelling of one of the settings and *Windows may not run at all.*

If you're using 640 by 480, and your hardware is made to support 800-by-600 resolution, you might want to compare higher resolutions of 640 by 480. For you *nuts-and-boltsy* types who like to do things the hard or manual way (in this case the easy way is using *Windows* Setup) here's a procedure for you computer dweebs—*without* using Setup.

1. Start Notepad.

2. Open the SYSTEM.INI. It's in your *Windows* directory.

3. Scroll down through the [boot] section until this line of text appears:

DISPLAY.DRV=VGA.DRV

4. To see what your monitor looks like in 800 by 600, you need to replace the text VGA.DRV with SUPER-VGA.DRV. You can't leave any spaces in the text. Save the file and close Notepad.

5. Now get out your *Windows* 3.1 diskettes. Look for the screen driver for 800-by-600 resolution called SUPERVGA.DR_. Copy SUPERVGA.DR_ to your WINDOWS\SYSTEM subdirectory.

6. The lion's share of your original *Windows* 3.1 files on your diskettes are in compressed format, so you need to expand your driver before you can use it. Find the file EXPAND.EXE on the same diskette that held the driver file (SUPERVGA.DR_). Copy EXPAND.EXE to the WINDOWS\SYSTEM subdirectory, as well.

7. Maximize Program Manager and select the File Run command from the menu. Next, we'll *expand* the compressed driver file. Type this next example of syntax into the Run text box, then press the Enter key or the OK button:

EXPAND.EXE SUPERVGA.DR_ SUPERVGA.DRV

8. *Windows* will have opened a DOS session and allowed EXPAND.EXE to complete the file-expansion process. Your 800-by-600 driver is now ready to use.

9. Make sure the Save Settings check box is checked in Program Manager, then leave and restart *Windows*.

If you replaced the text VGA.DRV with SUPERVGA.DRV, your screen now displays about 20 percent more than it did in 640-by-480 mode. Your group and other windows will not be displayed in the same areas of the screen as you may have become accustomed to under 640 by 480, so you'll need to rearrange your screen objects to suit yourself.

Of course, when you pack more pixels onto the same size screen, *Windows* makes everything appear smaller in the higher-resolution modes. You can now add more icons than you could in 640-by-480 mode, and view more of your open windows. This is the real impact of higher resolution. Everything is smaller (and harder to read) so you can get more onto your screen.

If you want to go back to the 640-by-480 mode, just run this procedure again, but replace SUPERVGA.DRV with VGA.DRV where it was in the [boot] section of your SYSTEM.INI file, and you're all done.

If you happen to have misspelled the line containing the driver name in the SYSTEM.INI file, *Windows* may beep during the next startup and stall with the *Windows* logo still on the screen. Just check your SYSTEM.INI file with a DOS-based text editor or use Setup from the DOS prompt to correct the error, or copy your saved version of SYSTEM.INI back to your WINDOWS/SYSTEM subdirectory and start the process over again (if you're not totally frustrated by this time).

If your hardware is not capable of the higher resolutions and you try this procedure anyway, you may get some pretty unpredictable results when *Windows* restarts. In this case, all you have to do is use a DOS-based text editor to open the SYSTEM.INI file and reinsert the statement DISPLAY.DRV=VGA.DRV in place of your most recent change to solve the problem.

Of course, to get yourself out of this little pickle, you can use *Windows* "Setup" from the DOS prompt as you did when you first installed *Windows*. Tell Setup you have a VGA monitor, and *Windows* takes care of the rest.

1024-by-768 or 8514/A Mode

If your monitor *and* video card are capable of displaying 1024-by-768 resolution, you should not install the driver that came with your video card the same way that you installed the 800-by-600 driver using the procedure given earlier.

You had best check the documentation that came with the video card's *Windows* screen drivers, and use *Windows* Setup to install the 1024-by-768 driver. The reason for this change is that *Windows* changes the way it displays screen fonts in this higher mode.

You will need the OEMSETUP.INF file included with your video card's driver diskette files as well as other files in order to display this mode of resolution. If you are not an advanced user, it's best to let *Windows* Setup work with the video card maker's INF file to install your *Windows* 1024-by-768 driver. If you're like me, you'll find that 8514/A on a 14-inch monitor is less than useful.

Even if your monitor is non-interlaced, the characters in 1024 mode are simply much too small on the icon titles to be easily readable. Try this resolution on your monitor and you may go back to 800 by 600 (alias *SVGA*), my favorite because I can get more on the screen than in 640-by-480 (*VGA*) mode.

It's often recommend that you try using 1024-by-768 mode only if you have a 16-inch (or larger is even better) non-interlaced monitor. It's just too much clutter and mumbo-jumbo on a standard 14-inch monitor of any type or model.

Don't forget something else: When you pack more pixels onto a screen, *Windows* and your video card have more variables (pixels) to manage, so your system seems to slow down a lot.

Here's the upside story. If you're using a 264-color screen driver in 640-by-480 mode, you can go to a 16-color 800-by-600 mode without much of a change in video refresh speed. In other words, there should *not* be a major difference in how fast you can scroll text files in a document. You should work with the change in resolution in the application where you spend most of your time to get a real feel for the added benefits of using another resolution. More colors are prettier, but I can't stand to add any waiting regardless of the scenery.

Most people who write for a living stick to 16-color drivers at any resolution because they don't really need 264 colors to generate documents, and they want all of the text-scrolling speed they can get.

Hardware Enhancements

There are a lot of video cards intended for *Windows* users these days. Most use the popular S3 and Sierra RAMDAC HiColor chipset to increase refresh rates—especially for *Windows* users.

Video card makers are finally responding to the needs of text mechanics like myself. Weitek, the maker of the famed math coprocessors, has developed a video card that is accelerated with its own video coprocessor. The card is called Weitek Power for *Windows*. Its particular claim to fame is that it's designed to increase video performance for *Windows* users in a very *specific* way. It's actually designed to apply most of its muscle power to graphical text-intensive tasks. In fact, the card is intended to accelerate *Windows* text-scrolling speed by up to 500 percent. I use one on my machine with great results. But then, I work almost exclusively with *words*.

If you suspect that your video card is a real slug compared to your system, try this simple test:

1. From the Program Manager's File menu, select Exit *Windows*.

2. When the Exit *Windows* dialog box appears, note the position of the OK button on the screen with your mouse pointer.

3. Leave your mouse pointer at the point on the screen where the pointer would have to be to hit the OK button the next time *this* dialog box appears.

4. Use the Tab key to switch the highlight to the Cancel button on the Exit *Windows* dialog box, then press the Enter key to clear the Exit *Windows* dialog box and restore the Program Manager. Remember, don't disturb the position of the mouse pointer!
5. Now use the keyboard to exit *Windows* (Alt-F, then X)... but *tap* the left mouse button a nanosecond after you hit the X key.

If *Windows* exits without displaying the Exit *Windows* dialog box again, your system is leaving *Windows* before your video card can complete the posting of the Exit *Windows* dialog box. You are probably going to get a substantial benefit from an accelerated video card designed for *Windows* users.

If you work with words primarily, the Weitek Power for *Windows* may be for you. If your work is centered on graphics, you may find that the ATI Ultra series of video boards increase your productivity substantially. The key word is *productivity*. When you're choosing a video card made to perform for *Windows* users, look into what it does well. They all differ somewhat in how they excel, and the prices can vary *a lot* when it comes down to price/performance measurement doing particular tasks!

Swapfile Virtues

If you're a *Windows* power-user, a "permanent swapfile" is an absolute must. That is, if you use *Windows* in '386 enhanced mode. Even if you can only afford to create a swapfile that is only 1 or 2 megabytes in size, you'll get an increase in *Windows* applications' performance that you will not want to go without once you've experienced it.

The size of the swapfile you create is directly related to the amount of memory you have in your system. A swapfile is an exercise in virtual memory. In this case, you are creating an extension of your system's memory on your hard drive. Yes it's incredibly sluggish memory because it is located on a mechanical device, but it's better than running out of memory when you are in the middle of doing something very important.

Windows begins to use this swapfile instead of memory when it senses that you have used your available memory. You'll know it when it happens. You'll think your system is crawling when it has to access your swapfile just to do what you ask of it.

In a nutshell, a swapfile is just a dedicated, large, permanent but empty file for *Windows* to access when it runs out of memory. For example, when a *Windows* program opens a file, and it finds it hasn't enough memory to complete loading the file or files into memory, it may place files that are not needed at that moment into the permanent holding area. This dedicated holding area is called a *swapfile*. Since *Windows* needs to work with virtual memory that is contiguous, you need to create a swapfile only after you have defragmented and compressed your hard drive. In fact, you should do these two things immediately before you install *Windows* for this very reason.

When you create a permanent swapfile, you in effect dedicate a portion of your hard drive. Permanent swapfiles must be kept in the same place at all times. *Windows* looks for the location of your permanent swapfile when it loads. If you've moved or erased it, *Windows* will give you holy heck and tell you that you'd better make a new one *or else*! Trust me, make a new one. Don't quibble.

The speed benefit to a permanent swapfile is simply one derived from common sense. Remember how we said that the permanent swapfile is not movable? In fact, it has file attributes of *system/hidden/archive*. DOS will not let you move it—much less find it—without a struggle.

The system attribute renders it unmovable. The hidden attribute makes it invisible from the DOS prompt so you're less likely to fudge it up, at least using DOS alone.

If *Windows* does not have to ask your hard drive to find a contiguous area when it needs to save a file or files to the virtual memory (the swapfile), it saves a *lot* of time in the process.

The existence of the permanent swapfile makes the process of extending your system's memory to your hard drive possible, and the fact that the swapfile is permanent *and* unmovable makes the use of it fast.

How Much Is Enough?

The size of your permanent swapfile really depends on how much memory you need, and what you are using for peripheral hardware. *Windows* will recommend a size for your swapfile based on how much memory it senses you have, and how much free space you have on your hard drive. First, let's talk about memory.

If you have the minimum memory to run *Windows* 3.1 in '386 enhanced mode (2 MB), you should create at least a 4-megabyte swapfile. I would be tempted to create a *at least* a 4-meg swapfile. If you have 4–8 megabyte memory capacity, you don't need quite so large a swapfile, because you are less likely to run out of memory, and therefore will probably not use the permanent swapfile that often. If you have 4–8 megs of memory, you might want to make a swapfile of maybe 2 megabytes.

A lot of programs you can use from *Windows* want differing sizes of swapfiles for their own reasons. Graphics applications utilize swapfiles a lot because they scan documents and images and load them into your system's memory for you to manipulate. A letter-size document may take more than 6 megabytes of memory, depending on the resolution you use when you scan the page. These programs will demand swapfile or virtual memory capacity that will make the swapfile size determination for you.

Many new hardware devices intended for use under *Windows* have their own requirements. For example, one such device is the LaserMaster WinPrinter 800. This printer uses your system memory and processor to print 400-dpi files and 800-dpi PostScript tasks. This machine is not for the faint-of-resource for this reason.

You need a '386, 8 megabytes of system memory and an 8-megabyte permanent swapfile just to install the printer on your system. The machine has little in the way of its own electronics except for the interface card that is placed in one of your system slots. The printer dumps an 800-dpi document into its paper catcher in about 30 to 45 seconds.

Just in case you're not up on PostScript printer performance, this is about one-quarter to one-fifth of the time needed to produce the same document on the competition's machines at *lower resolutions*. It can do so, because it uses your computer's CPU, coprocessor (if you have one) and memory (both real and virtual) to do much of its job. It needs a large permanent swapfile on your hard drive so it has a place to store large PostScript files while it's printing.

The LaserMaster WinPrinter 800 is just one example of the new breed of hardware devices that rely on the permanent swapfile and other system resources. Expect more reliance on your permanent swapfile in the future, as more and more hardware makers tap into this resource called *virtual memory*.

Appendix

Appendix
All About ASCII Characters

Control Characters

These are the characters produced by holding down the <Ctrl> key and simultaneously hitting another key. The number before each character is the decimal value the computer has assigned that character. With a different decimal value for each character, the computer won't become confused between <m>, <M>, and <^M>, for instance. (The caret symbol, ^, represents the <Ctrl> key.) To create any of the characters in these tables, you can type in the decimal number with the keypad while holding down the <Alt> key. See Chapter Five for more details.

Control characters aren't part of the alphabet. Instead, they're used as signals to tell the software what to do. Pushing <^K> for instance, can pull up a word processing menu.

0	^@	1	^A	2	^B	3	^C	4	^D	5	^E	6	^F	7	^G
8	^H	9	^I	10	^J	11	^K	12	^L	13	^M	14	^N	15	^O
16	^P	17	^Q	18	^R	19	^S	20	^T	21	^U	22	^V	23	^W
24	^X	25	^Y	26	^Z	27	^[	28	^\	29	^]	30	^^	31	^_

Standard Text Characters

These are the characters you'll see in your documents. They're the alphabet, the numbers, and a few common symbols. What's the character accessed by the blank left next to number 32? That's the spacebar!

32		33	!	34	π	35	#	36	$	37	%	38	&	39	'
40	(	41	)	42	*	43	+	44	,	45	-	46	.	47	/
48	0	49	1	50	2	51	3	52	4	53	5	54	6	55	7
56	8	57	9	58	:	59	;	60	<	61	=	62	>	63	?
64	@	65	A	66	B	67	C	68	D	69	E	70	F	71	G
72	H	73	I	74	J	75	K	76	L	77	M	78	N	79	O
80	P	81	Q	82	R	83	S	84	T	85	U	86	V	87	W
88	X	89	Y	90	Z	91	[	92	\	93	]	94	^	95	_
96	`	97	a	98	b	99	c	100	d	101	e	102	f	103	g
104	h	105	i	106	j	107	k	108	l	109	m	110	n	111	o
112	p	113	q	114	r	115	s	116	t	117	u	118	v	119	w
120	x	121	y	122	z	123	{	124			125	}	126	~	127	⌂

Extended ASCII Characters

Here you'll find your foreign characters. They'll change according to what "code page" you've assigned to your country setting. (See Chapter Five.)

128	Ç	129	ü	130	é	131	â	132	ä	133	à	134	å	135	ç
136	ê	137	ë	138	è	139	ï	140	î	141	ì	142	Ä	143	Å
144	É	145	æ	146	Æ	147	ô	148	ö	149	ò	150	û	151	ù
152	ÿ	153	Ö	154	Ü	155	¢	156	£	157	¥	158	₧	159	ƒ
160	á	161	í	162	ó	163	ú	164	ñ	165	Ñ	166	ª	167	º
168	¿	169	⌐	170	¬	171	½	172	¼	173	¡	174	«	175	»
176	░	177	▒	178	▓	179	│	180	┤	181	╡	182	╢	183	╖
184	╕	185	╣	186	║	187	╗	188	╝	189	╜	190	╛	191	┐
192	└	193	┴	194	┬	195	├	196	─	197	┼	198	╞	199	╟
200	╚	201	╔	202	╩	203	╦	204	╠	205	═	206	╬	207	╧
208	╨	209	╤	210	╥	211	╙	212	╘	213	╒	214	╓	215	╫
216	╪	217	┘	218	┌	219	█	220	▄	221	▌	222	▐	223	▀
224	∝	225	β	226	Γ	227	π	228	Σ	229	σ	230	µ	231	τ
232	Φ	233	Θ	234	Ω	235	δ	236	∞	237	φ	238	∈	239	∩
240	≡	241	±	242	≥	243	≤	244	⌠	245	⌡	246	÷	247	≈
248	°	249	∙	250	·	251	√	252	ⁿ	253	²	254	■	255	

All About ASCII Characters

Control Character Names

You'll probably never need to know these, but they're handy to have. For instance, Decimal 7, <^G>, and BEL are "Bell," or the "beep" you hear when you do something wrong. To hear the beep, type ECHO <^G> at the DOS prompt and hit <Enter>. Your computer will beep.

Similarly, you can control your printer using the ECHO trick and some of these characters.

```
 0  ^@  NUL  Null                  16  ^P  DLE  Data Link Escape
 1  ^A  SOH  Start of Heading      17  ^Q  DC1  Device Control 1
 2  ^B  STX  Start of Text         18  ^R  DC2  Device Control 2
 3  ^C  ETX  End of Text           19  ^S  DC3  Device Control 3
 4  ^D  EOT  End of Transmission   20  ^T  DC4  Device Control 4
 5  ^E  ENQ  Enquiry               21  ^U  NAK  Negative Acknowledgement
 6  ^F  ACK  Acknowledge           22  ^V  SYN  Synchronous File
 7  ^G  BEL  Bell                  23  ^W  ETB  End of Transmission Block
 8  ^H  BS   Backspace             24  ^X  CAN  Cancel
 9  ^I  HT   Horizontal Tab        25  ^Y  EM   End of Medium
10  ^J  LF   Line Feed             26  ^Z  SUB  Substitute
11  ^K  VT   Vertical Tab          27  ^[  ESC  Escape
12  ^L  FF   Form Feed             28  ^\  FS   Form Separator
13  ^M  CR   Carriage Return       29  ^]  GS   Group Separator
14  ^N  SO   Shift Out             30  ^^  RS   Record Separator
15  ^O  SI   Shift In              31  ^_  US   Unit Separator
```

For more information about ASCII characters, check out Dan Gookin's *DOS Secrets*. You'll find ordering information in the back of this book.

Index

Index

'386 enhanced mode, 117
386MAX, 3

A

Advanced MS-DOS Programming, 57
ANSI.SYS, 19
ASCII, 61, 151
   control characters, 151
   extended characters, 152
   standard text characters, 151
assembly language, 53
ATTRIB, 40
attributes, 40

B

BACKUP.EXE, 94, 103
batch files, 101
   AUTOEXEC.BAT menu, 105
   backup checking, 103
   formatting disks, 101
   moving files, 102
BBS
   calling, 75
bits per second (bps), 74
BMP, 120

C

CED (Command EDitor), 23
CHKDSK, 89
Clipboard, 125
   clearing, 128
   Clipboard Viewer, 125
   contents, 126
   files, 127
   uses for, 129
Collage Plus, 70
communications, 73
control characters, 151, 153
coprocessor, 16
CrossTalk, 75

CTTY, 75
   for security, 77

D

data word format, 74
DEBUG, 53
   creating a program script, 54
   debugging, 58
   programming in, 53
device drivers, 10
   ANSI.SYS, 19
DEVICEHIGH, 12
dialog boxes, 124
DIR, 43
directory ordering, 91
disaster recovery, 31
   MIRROR, 31
disk compaction, 90
disk partitions, 35
DoDot, 70
DOS
   function calls, 57
   programming in, 57
DOSEDIT, 23
DOSKEY, 23
   command line history, 24
   editing commands, 26
   macros, 27
   multiple commands, 26
   reviewing commands, 25
DOSKEY macros, 28
DOSSHELL
   HELP, 111
dot, 61

E

Editor, 20
EDLIN, 20
environment space, 130
extended ASCII characters, 152
extended memory, 5

F

FDISK.COM, 35
file compression, 91
file format conversion, 69
files
   backing up, 94
   batch, 101
   Clipboard, 127
   compression, 91
   format, 69
   hiding, 39
   securing, 39, 44
   self-erasing junk, 51
   viewing, 43
foreign characters, 152
FORMAT.COM, 97
free memory, 7
function calls, 57
function key codes, 22

G

general protection fault, 7
graphical computing, 115
graphics
   modes and standards, 62
   printing, 66
   translation utilities, 68
graphics mode, 61
GRAPHICS.COM, 65, 71

H

hard drive, 89
   cache, 90
   rules of thumb, 89
hardware
   compatibility, 2
   enhancements for *Windows*, 144
hardware memory, 1
HELP, 109
   DOSSHELL, 111
hexadecimal, 53
   chart, 54

hidden files, 39
high memory, 12
HIMEM.SYS, 4, 11
HotShot Graphics, 69
housekeeping, 93

J

junk files, 51

K

keyboard
   ANSI.SYS, 19
   enhancement, 19
   reassigning keys, 20

L

Lantastic, 78
LIM, 2
LOADHIGH, 12

M

Mace Utilities, 93
macros, 27
MEM.EXE, 7
memory
   conventional, 2, 8
   expanded, 5
   extended, 5
   free, 7
   hardware, 1
   high, 12
   management, 1
   upper, 8
   Windows, 136
memory management, 1
   HIMEM.SYS, 11
Micrografx Designer, 68
MIRROR, 31
MODE, 63, 82
modem, 73
   connecting, 73

Index

N
Norton Utilities, 93

P
Paintbrush, 120
partition table, 36
partitions, 35
PC Graphics, 61
PCTools, 93
pixel, 61
PKZIP, 91
Print Screen key, 67
printing, 81
    control in Editor, 85
    from DOS, 81
    graphics, 66
    GRAPHICS.COM, 67
    printer setup, 82
    with DOS, 83
Procomm, 75
program loaders, 3
programs
    loading, 15

R
RAM disk, 47
    example, 51
    installing, 48
    setup, 47
RAMDRIVE, 48
real mode, 116

S
screen capture, 70
    utilities, 70
screen dump, 65
scroll box, 123
SideKick, 11
SMARTDrive, 90
standard mode, 116
standard text characters, 151
swapfile, 145

SYSEDIT.EXE, 120
SYSTEM.INI, 120

T
TEMP, 93
terminal emulation, 75
text mode, 61
Tiffany+, 70
translation utilities, 68
TSR, 7, 10, 133

U
UMA, 3
    EMM386.EXE, 16
UNDELETE.EXE, 33
undeleting files, 33
UNFORMAT.COM, 34
unformatting, 34
upper memory area (UMA), 3

V
virtual memory, 148

W
wallpaper, 119
    making your own, 120
Weitek coprocessor, 16
WIN.INI, 120
Windows, 115
    '386 enhanced mode, 117
    1024-by-768 mode, 143
    800-by-600 mode, 140
    8514/A mode, 143
    changing DOS prompt, 130
    clipboard, 125
    controlling windows, 119
    data transfer, 135
    dialog boxes, 124
    DOS modes, 131
    DOS prompt icon, 129
    DOS TSRs, 133
    environment space, 130

general protection fault, 7
graphical computing, 115
hardware enhancements, 144
maximizing, 123
memory usage, 136
minimizing, 124
modes, 116
moving windows, 122
non-*Windows* tasks, 135
opening windows, 122
real mode, 116
recessing, 122
resolution, 139
scroll box, 123
scrolling, 122
secrets, 115
standard mode, 116
swapfiles, 145
switching programs, 138
tips, 137
utilities, 134
virtual memory, 148
wallpaper, 119
working with DOS, 129

Z

Zenographics Import, 69

Other Books From
Computer Publishing Enterprises:

PC Secrets
Tips and Tricks to Increase Your Computer's Power
by R. Andrew Rathbone

Future Computer Opportunities
Visions of Computers Into the Year 2000
by Jack Dunning

Software Buying Secrets
by Wally Wang

DOS Secrets
by Dan Gookin

101 Computer Business Ideas
by Wally Wang

Digital Dave's Computer Tips and Secrets
A Beginner's Guide to Problem Solving
by Roy Davis

The Best FREE Time-Saving Utilities for the PC
by Wally Wang

How to Get Started With Modems
by Jim Kimble

How to Make Money With Computers
by Jack Dunning

Rookie Programming
A Newcomer's Guide to Programming in BASIC, C, and Pascal
by Ron Dippold

Hundreds of Fascinating and Unique Ways to Use Your Computer
by Tina Rathbone

The Computer Gamer's Bible
by R. Andrew Rathbone

Beginner's Guide to DOS
by Dan Gookin

Computer Entrepreneurs
People Who Built Successful Businesses Around Computers
by Linda Murphy

How to Understand and Buy Computers
By Dan Gookin

Parent's Guide to Educational Software and Computers
by Lynn Stewart and Toni Michael

The Official Computer Widow's (and Widower's) Handbook
by Experts on Computer Widow/Widowerhood

For more information about these books, call 1-800-544-5541.